YOUNG PEOPLE
TALK ABOUT
DEATH

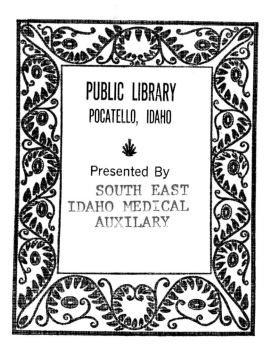

MARY McHUGH

YOUNG PEOPLE TALK ABOUT DEATH

Franklin Watts
New York/London/Toronto/Sydney
1980

Library of Congress Cataloging in Publication Data

McHugh, Mary.
Young people talk about death.

Bibliography: p.
Includes index.
SUMMARY: Presents opinions and experiences of
young people concerning death, aging, prolonging
life by extraordinary means, suicide, burial, cremation, explaining death to children, and what happens when one dies.
1. Death—Juvenile literature. 2. Death—Social as-
pects—Juvenile literature. 3. Children and death—
Juvenile literature. [1. Death] I. Title.
HQ1073.M32   301.42'86   79-24266
ISBN 0-531-02884-4

CONTENTS

Acknowledgments

I would like to thank the hundreds of high school students and their teachers who contributed their thoughts on death and dying to my book. I am especially grateful to the following people for their help: Mr. Robert Stevenson, who teaches "Perspectives on Death" at River Dell High School in Oradell, N.J.; Mr. John Surak, who also teaches a course on death at Waldwick High School in Waldwick, N.J.; Mr. Angelo Caruso and Mr. Thomas Freeswick, Social Science teachers at Ramapo High School in Franklin Lakes, N.J.; Mr. David Alwine, a teacher at Radnor High School in Radnor, Pa.; and Mrs. Reed Shoemaker, Head of the Baldwin School in Bryn Mawr, Pa.

YOUNG PEOPLE TALK ABOUT DEATH

CHAPTER I
INTRODUCTION

No one really believes he is going to die. We are so insulated from death and dying in this country that most of us avoid thinking about it or talking about it. Many of us have never seen a dead person. Grandparents die in hospitals or nursing homes now instead of upstairs in their own beds. The minute they die, they are whisked off to a room out of sight of other patients and visitors.

When our country was mainly a rural society, death was as much a part of life as the birth of a baby. Animals died, grandparents died, children died. There was no mystery about death because it was so familiar. Neighbors came to help prepare the body for burial, and children visited the dying with their parents to say goodbye. When a child asked, "Where did grandma go?" the answer was "To heaven to be with God."

Today we have no simple answers to that question, but at least we are beginning to talk about death again, to take away some of the mystery that surrounds it. In the last five to ten years, death has come out of the closet and is being studied by thanatologists, as well as by psychologists, psychiatrists, social workers, sociologists, doctors, and nurses. Many high school and college teachers, too, are taking a new, open, questioning attitude toward death, and to find out what effect this is having on young people, I talked to hundreds of students and asked them for their opinions. You will find their comments throughout this book.

One of the strongest influences in our society is television. TV has exposed us to homosexuality, adultery, abortion, child abuse, transvestism, battered wives, rape, menopause, and many other previously forbidden subjects. Now death, too, can be discussed. Whether a panel of experts talks about teenage suicide or Mary Tyler Moore attends a funeral for Chuckles the Clown, the subject is no longer taboo.

Another powerful influence in changing our attitude toward death is Dr. Elisabeth Kubler-Ross, a Swiss-born psychiatrist now working in California. Her book, *On Death and Dying*, has led to workshops and seminars on the subject all over the country. Dr. Kubler-Ross found that dying patients were often ignored and neglected by doctors and nurses. She began to pay special attention to these people, and she learned that they wanted to talk about their impending death. They welcomed the chance to discuss their fears with her.

When she asked other doctors to point out terminally-ill patients to her so that she might help them, she met fierce resistance from physicians who believed that people wanted to be left alone when they were dying. Gradually, Dr. Kubler-Ross managed to persuade some members of the medical community to change their attitude toward the terminally ill and their relatives. Nurses, especially, have been responsive to this idea. Doctors, however, are slower to accept her findings and are often reluctant to attend seminars on death and dying.

During her work with patients, Dr. Kubler-Ross noticed a pattern of reactions and identified five stages of dying: denial, anger, bargaining, withdrawal, and acceptance. Not a neat, orderly sequence of emotions, the five stages appear and disappear, then reappear during the process of dying. Often, though, the person who finds out he or she is dying denies the fact at first. "The tests must be wrong." Or "I'll get a second opinion." Then, when it is clear that the tests are not wrong, when the second doctor agrees with the first, the person becomes angry—really angry at being cheated out of a longer life, but to others, he or she seems angry at them.

"I couldn't understand why my father was so angry at my mother and me when he was dying," one high school junior told me. "When I read Dr. Kubler-Ross' book, I finally understood why—it was a normal part of dying."

Nurses and doctors, too, are now better prepared for the anger directed at them by dying patients. "I used to stay away from terminally-ill people as much as possible," said a young nurse in a New York hospital. "Now I give them a chance to talk out their anger, their frustrations. I listen to them."

Either before, during, or after anger comes the bargaining stage. "Just let me live until my daughter graduates from law school," or "until my first grandchild is born." And oddly enough, many people will tell you a story about a relative who did live until a granddaughter got married or a son graduated from college.

The next stage is withdrawal, a pulling away from one's family. This is a necessary step toward acceptance of death, but relatives are often hurt during this part of the process. If they understood that it was a natural stage, they would let the person go. To say, "You'll be all right," or "When you get home, we'll take that trip to California," is to prevent the patient's acceptance of death. There are people who deny death until the end, but with most people, the last stage—acceptance—is finally reached.

A dying patient may resent the categorizing of his or her emotions by others. Ted Rosenthal, a young poet who died of leukemia, appeared in a film called "How Could I Not Be Among You." He tells us in vividly honest words exactly what his last months are like. With humor and painful accuracy, he describes his reactions to the nurses' and doctors' acceptance of his various moods and emotions.

"All those people that tell you you're predictable, and that you'll die in the same way everybody else does are right. At first I resented him saying, 'Oh, you're at the angry stage' or 'Three and a half weeks from now you'll feel lost.' Well, they're right. I'm following the guidelines for terminal cancer patients down to the letter. It's fiendish. No matter what I say, they say, 'Mm-hmmm, that's what we thought you'd say.' "

The most important result of Dr. Kubler-Ross' work has been to clear the way for a completely new examination of death and the way we treat the terminally ill. Through her efforts, many hospitals now offer grief counseling to the dying and to their relatives. Dr. Kubler-Ross' books, including: *On Death and Dying, Questions and Answers on Death and Dying,* and *Death: the Final Stage of Growth,* are used as basic texts for hundreds of seminars and courses at universities and hospitals all over the country. She has also helped to spread the word about the hospice movement over here. In the Middle Ages the word *hospice* meant a place to rest during a journey. Now, as redefined by St. Christopher's Hospice near London, a hospice is a resting place for people who are making their final journey. In this country, hospice teams of specially trained nurses, doctors, social workers, and psychologists keep the terminally ill comfortable and as happy as possible until their death. They remind us that the dying are not already dead. In Chapter III, you will find more detailed information about this movement.

Dr. Kubler-Ross' work with children who have lost a parent or who are dying themselves has shown us a new way to deal with the pain. Believing that we can all come to terms with death if we face it, confront our guilt and overcome it, she travels all over the country to counsel the dying without charge.

This remarkable woman also discovered a phenomenon quite by accident as she interviewed dying patients. She found a surprising similarity in the stories told to her by people who had been pronounced dead by doctors and were then revived. Her findings paralleled those of Dr. Raymond A. Moody who wrote a book called *Life After Life* about his own patients' experiences with near death. The controversy sparked by the strangely similar reports of long tunnels, a figure they called God, or Christ, or Love, according to their religious background, and a review of all the events in their lives, from people of widely disparate backgrounds and religions is reflected in the avid interest of the teenagers who told me their own opinions of these studies in Chapter VIII.

Because of Dr. Kubler-Ross' findings, more and more teachers are introducing the subject of death and dying into their classrooms. A few high schools offer a mini-course on death to their juniors and seniors as an elective. The majority, however, include a unit on death and dying in other courses, such as English, sociology, psychology, or health education. Colleges, too, offer courses and seminars on death to undergraduates and graduates.

When I talked to high school juniors and seniors and college students and asked them to discuss topics related to death and dying, my first question was, "How do you feel when you hear the word

death?" Their answers reflected the wide range of
attitudes in our society as a whole:

Fear:

- "The scariest thing is that life keeps going on without
  you. You can't wake up in the morning. I like being
  alive."

- "People are afraid of death because they don't know
  what's waiting for them afterward."

  "We're high school seniors, and I think that's why
  death scares us so much—because there's so much
  ahead of us."

- "It's *how* you die that's frightening. I'm afraid of
  suffering, of being half dead and half alive for months
  in the hospital."

  "Death is the ultimate in fear because no one understands it. It's the only thing man can never find out."

  "Death scares me, but at the same time it intrigues
  me—I want to know what happens afterward."

Denial:

"My grandmother is dying, but she doesn't talk about
her death. She talks about what will happen to her
collection of demitasse cups."

"When I talk about death to my friends, they sort of

smile, but it's extremely rare that anybody talks about it."

～"People in this country tend to avoid people who aren't 'normal,' whether they're dying or crippled or blind. They don't like to talk about it or be reminded of it."

"I see no reason to think of it now. Death is an ending of life, and right now, I'm just beginning. I don't think we should depress ourselves by thinking about it."

"By the time I'm old enough to die, they'll have found a way to keep people from dying."

Acceptance:

"If you've seen animals copulate and die on a farm, you understand that these things are a part of nature, and that humans do everything animals do, but when you live in a society that hides these things from you, protects you from them, how can you understand them?"

"The first time the goldfish you bought at the fair dies, the first time you try to save a leaf from turning brown, you realize the transience of all things in our world. Gradually you know you will die too."

"In Hamlet the gravediggers matter-of-factly dig up one grave, taking out the remains and putting a new body in. That's all it really is—out and in, out and in."

"I try to keep my death close to me all the time by

thinking I could die any time. The closer I can come to my death, the more intensely I can live now. It's like a deadline on a paper—you work harder the day before it's due."

"Any transition is difficult. A baby is warm and comfortable inside the womb and doesn't want to come out. Then when you get used to this life, you don't want to leave."

Religious:

"Religion helps comfort you. Most people have a religion because they're afraid to die. It tells you how to live your life so you will go to heaven when you die. It's better for me to know there's a place for me afterward, that everything I've done on earth, all of my work, wasn't just for nothing."

"I'm not scared of death. I guess it's because of my religion. You know—you look forward to the afterlife."

Non-religious:

"They invented religion to get rid of their fears. They just use it as a cop-out. It's all based on the fact that nobody knows."

"When I'm really scared, I almost believe there's a God, but deep down, I don't really believe there's another life after this one."

Wish for immortality:

"If I could leave something behind, I would achieve some sort of immortality—the creation of a child or some art form. That would make death a little more acceptable."

"It's not easy talking about dying when you're young. As one high school junior said, "I realize *intellectually* that I'm going to die, but it's not real to me. People don't die at seventeen."

But unfortunately, people do die at seventeen—from automobile accidents, drug abuse, cancer, and much too often, from suicide. Suicide is the second leading cause of death among people between fifteen and twenty-four. I asked the students I interviewed to tell me why they think so many of their peers choose to end their lives, and you will find their answers in Chapter V.

Our changing attitude toward death, plus technological advances which allow doctors to prolong life, have resulted in new ethical and moral problems for doctors: Is a person dead when the heart stops or when the brain stops functioning? Should a person be kept alive by a respirator when there is no brain wave activity? Should the doctor tell a patient he or she is dying? Should doctors be allowed to turn off the respirator of a patient whose brain has died so they can take out the kidney to save the life of another? Should marijuana or other illegal drugs be used to alleviate the side effects of chemotherapy? Should a hopelessly deformed baby be kept alive? These problems are discussed in Chapter IV.

The young people I talked to had very strong feelings about funerals. Their comments ranged from "Funerals are the worst!" to "You can't treat your death as a matter of economy—funerals are important." In Chapter VI, you will find their opinions on funeral costs, burial versus cremation, and the use of land for cemeteries in an age when the living are running out of space.

In one high school class in Pennsylvania, a German exchange student said, "Americans think they can stop the process of death. They think if they try hard enough they can change anything." She may be right. There are scientists who believe we can slow down the aging process and replace parts that wear out, so that someday death will be almost obsolete. There are people who arrange to have their bodies frozen after death with the hope they can be brought back when the cure to their disease is discovered. Some people believe they will come back to live another life here on earth, and there are hypnotists who claim to have taken their subjects back to a former life. A discussion of what happens to you when you die according to other religions and cultures is included in Chapter VIII.

Trying to explain death to children is one of the most difficult tasks parents face. Some teenagers I talked to felt their parents had handled this distressing experience well, but many were still disturbed years later by feelings of guilt and terror at the hushed atmosphere surrounding death. They talked about how they would tell their own children in Chapter VII.

I found a real concern for the elderly among young people. Many had visited nursing homes and retirement homes to see a grandparent or as a volunteer, and they often expressed compassion for our older citizens. They were especially angry at society's tendency to treat old people like children. One high school senior said indignantly, "People always say, 'Oh, isn't that cute?' when they talk about active old people, as if it's really wonderful they can get around at their age." In Chapter III, some of the difficulties of growing old in this society are explored.

I was impressed with the thoughtful answers from the young people I interviewed for this book. There is certainly less reluctance to talk about death than I had expected, and I think you will find their discussions illuminating and honest.

CHAPTER II
TALKING ABOUT
DEATH

Since this book deals with the opinions and experiences of young people concerning death, I visited high schools and colleges where courses on death and dying are taught as electives, either as a mini-course or as a unit in sociology, psychology, and English classes, to ask students to tell me their personal experiences with death. Only recently have schools, especially secondary schools, recognized the need for such courses. A National Education Association publication, quoted in the March 16, 1978 *New York Times*, said, "The study of death is probably the last of the old taboos to fall in the schools. It is certainly not surprising that the subject should be one of the more recent arrivals in the curriculum, given Americans' distaste for consideration of it."

I sat in on some classes on death, and was impressed with the way teachers are handling this difficult subject. Robert Stevenson, a history teacher at River Dell High School in Oradell, New Jersey, teaches a nine-week elective course, "Perspectives on

Death," to juniors and seniors. He decided to initiate this course when he had trouble coping with the death of his own mother despite his having grown up as an Irish Catholic in New York, where he attended fifty or sixty wakes for relatives and family friends. "I began to think if death could hit me like that with my background and familiarity with death, what must it do to some of my students who have never in their whole lives lost anybody close to them. Many young people today have never seen a dead person, never been to a wake or lost anyone close to them. When I suggested this course to the Board [of Education], it was accepted and there is now a waiting list to take it."

Mr. Stevenson uses every device available to teach his students about death. He plays contemporary music. "Nine out of ten songs deal with death," he says. Kiss, Simon and Garfunkel, and Tom Paxton's "Forest Lawn," for example. "We discuss things like 'What can I do now that will make it easier for others when I'm gone?' We get into the nuts and bolts of life insurance. We talk about wills and the kids say, 'I have nothing to leave.' I remind them of things they own with little monetary value that they might want to give to someone. I show them how to write a will. We talk about funeral costs and visit a funeral parlor and crematorium. They write their own epitaphs, eulogies, obituaries; plan their own funerals. Some people who have had this course have taken charge of funeral arrangements for a family member when they were only eighteen or nineteen.

We discuss Dr. Kubler-Ross' five stages of death, children's perception of death, burial versus cremation. We decide who should be allowed in a bomb shelter when there isn't room for everyone—a mother of nine children or a man who has discovered the cure for cancer."

The course includes films, such as *All the Way Home, The Loved One, Eric, Death and Dying, Closing the Circle,* and *How Could I Not Be Among You.* Books he recommends include *About Dying* by Sarah Bonnet Stein, *A Death in the Family* by James Agee, *Sunshine* by Norma Klein, *Go Ask Alice,* anonymous, *Dreamland Lake* by Richard Peck, *Wild in the World* by John Donovan, *The Loners* by Nancy Garden, and, *Please Don't Go* by Peggy Woodford. For anybody considering starting such a course, there is a free *Study Guide for a Mini-course on Death,* offered by Avon Books, Education Department, 959 Eighth Avenue, New York, New York 10019.

Mr. Stevenson feels it is important to teach this subject in high school. To those who think high school students are too young to talk about death and that it should be taught in college, he says, "A lot of kids don't go to college. Don't they have a right to know these things, to expand their minds too?

"Sometimes I ask: Would you rather be a hangman, a member of a firing squad, or an executioner in a prison? Almost invariably they want to be on a firing squad or an executioner so they won't have to see the victim up close, face to face. With a firing squad, one gun has a blank so you never know if you were the one who killed the person. If you pull the switch on the electric chair, you're in another room.

"I teach my students to build memories while people they love are still alive. Memories don't just happen—you have to make them happen. My father died when I was a baby and the only thing I have left to remind me of him is one slide of my father, my mother, and me in my father's arms. It's important to take pictures, make tape recordings, capture moments that are important to you so you will have them later when people you love are gone. And I remind them that it is better to say 'I love you' once when someone can hear it than a thousand times when it's too late."

Every newspaper article, TV program, play, book, or film that deals with death is used in the course, which changes and grows as the subject becomes more and more accepted in our society. Fewer educators echo the dean of a girls' private school near Philadelphia who told me she could not allow any discussion of death in her school unless a psychiatrist were present. The value of open discussions on death and dying was proven by the comments made by students. One boy who had a horror of death didn't want to accompany the class on a visit to the funeral home, but Mr. Stevenson persuaded him to come along. A week later his grandmother died. He acted as one of the pall bearers at the funeral, and said he couldn't have done it if he hadn't taken the course.

Another boy whose father died was able to help

his mother understand the anger and withdrawal he had shown while he was dying. "My father died three years ago, and I didn't really understand why he acted the way he did before he died. I took the course to help me understand him better, and it did. I don't feel so bad now. We learned about the five stages of dying and I went home and told my mother about it, and she said she wished she could have taken the course too."

Susan, a senior, talked about how the course had helped her after her father's heart attack. "I was really afraid of my father's death. I needed reassurance and I needed to know more so I could face his death if he should die soon. I feel more at home with it since I talk about it every day in this course."

Another girl, Diane, expressed the value of the course in one sentence: "Life is more precious because I'm more aware of death now."

When high school and college students told me about their personal experiences with death, they emphasized the importance of talking about it. A senior at one high school in Connecticut told of his first confrontation with death:

"One summer when I was thirteen, I was working for my father in his construction business, and we were adding a room to a house which belonged to an older couple. I had just shaken hands with the owner of the house, when all of a sudden he fell on the floor with a heart attack. In the space of about seven minutes, the police had arrived, the ambulance was there, and he was dead. That was a real shock to me because just a second before I held his hand, and it was so strong. I could even feel his pulse. The next minute he was cold dead. He turned a different color. His eyes were really wide open, and the whole expression on his face was different.

"Luckily, in our house, we're really open with each other and we talk about death. If my parents hadn't been able to discuss it, I think it would really have hit me harder. I got it out of my system."

"I wish *my* family could talk about death," said Barbara, another student in that class. "When my grandfather died I was eleven or twelve. He lived in Israel, and my mother didn't tell me he had died for about six months. When I asked my mother why she waited so long, she said she thought I was too young, that she didn't want me to see how upset she was. I resented the fact that people were hiding things behind my back and that I had to find out about it through bits and pieces of conversation."

"After my brother died," said Anne, "I wanted to talk about his death, but there was nobody to talk to. It would be better if people said anything rather than pretending he never lived. He was such a part of my life and lots of times I want to talk about something we did together, but people give me that I-feel-so-sorry-for-you look."

In another school, a junior named Rick told me about his friend who was dying of cancer at nineteen. "He's already had two operations," he said. "He's on chemotherapy now, and you can see him deteriorating, but it's amazing just to talk to him. You would think talking to a person who is doomed would be really depressing, but he makes you appreciate your life so much more because he cherishes every minute he has left. He's not really talking about dying though. He talks about life, his life as it is right now: how everything looks better, how the air smells better, the grass looks greener."

A teenager in Chicago told this story about a friend of his:

"My friend's father was dying. My friend never really got along with him because he was very conservative. His father knew he was dying, and he started talking about the things he was afraid of, the things that he thought about, and in a way, started to show the poetic side of himself, his imaginative side which he had always hidden from his son. They came to an understanding which they never could have reached if they hadn't known it was their last chance."

Although Dr. Kubler-Ross found that dying patients yearn to talk about their own death, most people avoid the subject of death entirely with terminally ill friends and relatives. They talk about the weather, the vacation they would take as soon as the person recovered, the hospital food, anything but the impending death.

A few hospitals have instituted grief counseling,

or bereavement counseling, so that relatives of the dying as well as the dying can talk about their grief. This is a growing field for nurses, social workers, psychologists, and clergymen. Jim, a junior in a New York high school, told me how much this service had helped him when his sister was dying of leukemia.

"My mother, my sister, and I went through counseling with a woman psychologist who was trained as a grief therapist. It was more helpful than any relative or friend could have been. When you lose your sister it's like losing a part of yourself. It was something our family really never talked about before. At first the doctors thought if my sister knew she was dying, she'd just give up and die right then, but she lived four and a half years. My mother held her during counseling, rocking back and forth with her while the counselor tried to help my mother deal with me and my father.

"I was very mad at those people who never came to see my sister when she went into radiation therapy. Her hair fell out, she looked different, and they didn't want to see her. Then they came to the funeral and were hysterical."

In many hospitals today, parents of children with leukemia can talk to other parents whose children have the same disease. Group sessions are set up and parents are invited to join them if they wish. Most attend at least one session as a trial, and soon find the comments of other parents very helpful. If you have just found out your child has leukemia, it is comforting to hear another parent tell you about their daughter who has had leukemia for three years and is playing baseball every day.

There are other peer groups that help bereaved people: The Compassionate Friends, an international group which helps parents whose children have died; The Widowed Persons Service, sponsored by several organizations, which publishes the *Directory of Services for the Widowed in the United States and Canada*, a listing of names and locations of centers set up to help widows and widowers. Volunteers are trained to help these people cope with the problems that arise after the death of a spouse. It is especially helpful to widows who have depended on their husbands to handle all financial matters, and who suddenly find they must learn to take care of themselves. Besides there being legal, investment, and religious counselors available, other widows and widowers provide a sympathetic ear to ease the depression and fears that arise after the death of a spouse.

None of the teenagers I talked to could tell me what it was like to be actually dying, but a young poet named Ted Rosenthal spoke about it in his film, *How Could I Not Be Among You*.

"When they told me I had acute leukemia, I was confused, if anything. I called up countless people and said, 'Guess what's happening to me?' And everybody came over and kissed me and hugged me and loved me, but there was this undercurrent of despair underneath it all.

"I never really saw what fear was until I saw everybody else looking at me. I didn't feel any need for their sympathy. They just made me nervous. I realized that I wasn't frightened at all. I felt really good for the first time in my life. I had nothing to lose. Having nothing to lose, I could be anything.

"There's something about dying that separates you from all other people. Nobody can walk into death and walk back out the same person. You can live a lifetime in a day.

"I was a happier person once I became sick. I remember thinking, 'If only I could live and benefit from my present state of mind.' But when I was given more time to live, I lost the state of mind. You can't have it both ways. To live in the moment, you literally have to have a sense of having nothing to live for. Just realizing there's no real purpose to life and be able to live life fully from moment to moment.

"As soon as I was told I had a chance of surviving, that open rich feeling I had went crashing to the ground. I just got scared from that point on."

Apparently, Ted Rosenthal could not deal with the remission and the uncertainty of not knowing when he would die. He could cope with the sentence of "less than a year to live," but when he found out he would live for an indefinite period, he couldn't handle it and left his wife and children, moved 3,000 miles away from his family and died alone and in despair five years later.

CHAPTER III
GROWING OLD

"Mary," said my father one day when he was seventy-five, recuperating from an operation for cancer, "Don't ever get old." Considering the alternative, I decided to ignore his advice and live to be a hundred. If we're lucky, we'll all get old some day, and the problems of the elderly will be our problems before we know it.

In the past, half of our population died before the age of forty. Now, half live to be older than seventy. By the year 2000, there will be 30 million people over sixty-five, which means they will outnumber those under twenty-five. Half of those 30 million will be over seventy-five, putting them in the fastest growing age group in our country. Most people—almost 75 percent—die in nursing homes or hospitals among strangers. Families used to live together, with grandparents an important part of the home life, and most old people died at home. Now with families scattered all over the country, old people often die alone. If they live with their children, they often feel unwanted and a burden. If they live alone, a sudden illness could leave them helpless. If they live in a retirement home, they are often treated like children. The majority of nursing home residents are women since they outlive men four to one in this country.

There is a very high suicide rate among people over sixty-five—5,000 to 8,000 a year, and white men between seventy and seventy-four account for a large percentage of this number. Five times as many elderly men commit suicide as women. Dr. Adrian Ostfeld, Professor of Public Health at the Yale University School of Medicine, believes men in our society are used to being productive, useful people, and when they are deprived of valuable work, their self-respect and self-esteem are destroyed.*

I found young people very sympathetic to the plight of the aging in our society.

"This is really a country for young people," one high school student said. "People don't want to get old. In other societies old people are respected. Here they're treated like problem children. I belong to a singing group that goes to an old-age home and there are all those church ladies hovering around, baking cakes and teaching the old people to weave potholders. I can't stand it because they treat those people like babies. They should respect the elderly."

In China, a country with a long tradition of respect for the elderly, older people are useful, valued members of the community. Everyone in China

* *New York Times,* January 2, 1979, p. c-2.

works, and that includes the aged. People can retire as early as fifty, if they wish, but there is no mandatory retirement age. After retirement, the elderly are recruited to settle neighborhood disputes and to participate in the political life of the town. Their opinions are valued. However, lest you envision some utopia for the elderly, where everyone is busy, useful, and happy, some of the jobs assigned to old people are not exactly delightful. Old men are assigned the task of picking up papers and trash in the parks. Old women take care of the children in tiny, cramped quarters, where they must draw water from a source distant from the home, shop every day because there is no refrigeration, and wash the laundry by hand. But no one goes hungry and no one lacks health care.* The difference between living with your children and grandchildren in China and living in an upstairs bedroom in your daughter's house in America is the way you are treated. In China you are respected and deferred to. In America, you are often considered a nuisance and a burden.

One group that is working hard to change the national attitude toward the elderly is the Gray Panthers, a well-organized, efficient association with 107 chapters throughout the country, whose members include the young, the middle-aged, and the old. It was founded by Maggie Kuhn, now seventy-three years old, and five of her friends in 1970. Through vigorous lobbying, frequent TV appearances, and coalitions

* *The Gerontologist,* 1979, pp. 41-42.

with other groups, such as Ralph Nader's Retired Professional Action Group which published *Citizens' Guide for Nursing Home Reform*, Maggie and her group persuaded Congress to raise the mandatory retirement age to seventy. They also lobbied for a law which increased Social Security benefits 3 percent for each year a person works beyond sixty-five. They were responsible for the creation of the National Institute on Aging within the Department of Health, Education and Welfare, and the passage of a law against age discrimination in 1975. In 1978, a Comprehensive Older Americans Act became law, and in 1981 there will be a White House Conference on Aging.

Government programs such as the Foster Grandparents Program, Meals on Wheels, which supplies hot lunches for people who can't get out, and a retired senior volunteer program, are all results of efforts by the Gray Panthers and other citizens' groups.

The Foster Grandparents Plan, for instance, pays travel expenses and gives a small stipend to elderly retired people who work with retarded, emotionally disturbed, or other institutionalized children, and provides the love and care these children need.

Maggie Kuhn sees the problems of the elderly as problems for us all. She would welcome health care which would incorporate a more holistic, preventive approach to medicine. Besides free health care, she would like to see the American Medical Association approve more medical schools in the United States so there would be more doctors available to the growing elderly population as well as the rest of society, and she thinks medical schools should require courses on geriatrics and gerontology. Many diseases unique to the old are undiagnosed and untreated because doctors assume senility when the patient is really suffering from something else.

Only a small percentage of old people develop real senility. Temporary depression or confusion due to the loss of a spouse or other traumatic experience is often mistakenly diagnosed as senility. Dr. Robert Kastenbaum, who was at Wayne State University in Detroit at the time, conducted a study in which he produced symptoms of senility in young people when he speeded up an assigned task beyond their capacity to perform it. "Senile behavior is in large measure socially induced and can be created in anyone stripped of their roles, prestige, purpose, economic independence, and physical well-being," he says. "So-called senility is not age-dependent and is not inevitable with age." *

Because most Americans do equate age and senility, they are afraid of growing old. Dr. Walter Bortz, a professor at Stanford University Medical School, believes we could live to be one hundred and twenty with a little exercise and proper eating habits, but that most people don't want to live that long. "If I could convince you that to be eighty-five

* Robin M. Henig. "Exposing the Myth of Senility." *New York Times Magazine,* December 3, 1978, p. 158.

is really an exciting opportunity and that you will be valuable to yourself and others, then you would give up smoking, you'd run three times a week, you'd lose weight, and you'd live longer," he says.*

Ms. Kuhn would like to see the return of the old-fashioned family doctor who makes house calls and is concerned with the health of the whole family. Too few doctors are taught preventive medicine, she says. Nutrition, health education, responsibility for one's own health maintenance, and awareness of pollutants, are a neglected area of health care.** These are important to all of us, not just the elderly.

Maggie Kuhn sees the integration of young and old as a vital issue for the future. She herself lives in an old house in Philadelphia with three people in their twenties and thirties. "My role," she says, "is as a friend. I'm not some kind of surrogate parent or mother superior, and my housemates are not my surrogate children. . . . What I find rewarding in our situation is the mutuality, the give and take as equals. My housemates comfort and advise me, and I do the same for them. . . . I love the vitality of these young people; having them around re-energizes me, makes me feel more alive. What I have to offer them, hopefully, is a sense of experience and survivorship, which can help give perspective to their lives. These differ-

* *New York Times,* January 7, 1979.

** Margaret E. Kuhn. "Gray Panther Thoughts on Ageism, Health Care and Worklife." Unpublished essay.

ent qualities are the perennial qualities of the young and the old, and when exchanged in friendship they give richness to all concerned." *

Unfortunately, many communities make it difficult for such living arrangements to exist because of zoning laws which prohibit people not related to each other from living together in one house. This prevents many lonely old people and young people from enriching each others' lives in this way.

Too many older people choose to isolate themselves from the young. A high school junior in Massachusetts told me a typical story of her family's modern dilemma of what to do with Grandma.

"My family is in turmoil now," she said, "because my grandmother can't decide whether to keep on living with us or to go into an apartment by herself. She likes being with us kids. My little sister comes and plays the violin with her, and I love to talk to her about when my mother was a little girl. But she's also there for all the arguments and she gets involved with everything that happens. I think it would be better if she had her own place and we could come and visit her. She'd feel more independent and she'll be with people her own age."

Maggie Kuhn and the Gray Panthers disagree with this point of view. They encourage integration of the

* Margaret E. Kuhn. "Why Old and Young Should Live To-gether." *Gray Panther Network*, January 1979, p. 6.

generations, not isolation of the old in a retirement community while the young huddle together in housing developments. Both groups lose from this arrangement.

Ms. Kuhn's vision of the future includes a much more realistic blending of work and leisure lives. Young people are demanding opportunities for travel and study throughout their working lives, not just a trip to Europe after retirement. "Rather than seeing the end of mandatory retirement as the solution, we should consider a broad range of options that would make the structure of education, work, and leisure more flexible." Sabbatical leaves, part-time or shared work, and facilitating of mid-career changes, are all solutions proposed by Ms. Kuhn.*

In her zeal to improve life for the rest of us Maggie Kuhn travels all over the world, and to meet her is to stop worrying about the slowing down of physical and mental activity with aging. She radiates enthusiasm and intelligence and has no patience for the patronizing tolerance of the old. She combats stereotyped thinking by recommending and fighting for legislation and watching over Congressional hearings on topics related to the elderly. She traveled to China to study health care and the status of the aged there. She appears on television to berate depiction of older people as impotent, foolish, slow-thinking, physically debilitated nitwits.

* Margaret E. Kuhn. "Gray Panther Thoughts on Ageism, Health Care and Worklife." Unpublished essay.

The greatest worry of the elderly is what will happen to them if they should be ill for a long period before their death. All of us worry about a lingering, painful terminal illness, and there is a growing hospice movement in this country which can alleviate some of those fears.

This is a method of caring for the dying developed by Dr. Cicely Saunders in 1967 at St. Christopher's Hospice near London. There are forty such groups in England and hundreds in existence in America. The doctors, nurses, social workers, and clergymen associated with hospices work as teams in hospitals or people's homes to provide patients with the special kind of care needed by the terminally ill.

The purpose of hospice treatment is to help the patient live as comfortably and as fully as possible until he or she dies. An essential ingredient of this care is the use of medication which keeps the person pain-free but still alert and able to function. No one has to wait an hour in pain for relief. Medication is available before the pain becomes too severe. In England they use a mixture called Brompton's Cocktail, which contains heroin, cocaine, alcohol, flavored syrup, and chloroform water. Here, because heroin and cocaine are illegal, we substitute morphine.

"It's very important that patients are not treated like little children who have nothing to say," Dr. Kubler-Ross said in an interview on the NBC show, "Tomorrow." "They know how much pain they have and they don't have to wait an additional half hour in terrible agony. To die with dignity is to die in character, to have some control over where it happens and how comfortable you want to be, and that you're not doped up and can talk."

Everything is done to make life pleasant. Family members and friends are encouraged to visit, especially children. The atmosphere is cheerful. Beauticians come in regularly to help women feel attractive. There are birthday parties and activities intended to enhance daily living. It's just the opposite of the neglect most dying people suffer in hospitals. Patients are treated as valuable adults, cherished until their very last minute on earth. They are encouraged to return home when the management of the symptoms makes that possible. Most people, if given the choice, would rather die at home, and hospice care includes home treatment as well as in-patient care. The patient's family, too, is an important part of this type of treatment, and their physical and emotional needs are also met by the specially-trained staff. The stress of losing someone we love can make the grieving person more susceptible to illness, and the hospice team watches over the family's physical health as well as their emotional well-being. Hospices are planned in many states, and will be the ideal places for the terminally ill. Information about hospices in your area can be obtained by writing to: Hospice, Inc., 765 Prospect Street, New Haven, Connecticut 06511.

CHAPTER IV
MORAL AND
ETHICAL DILEMMAS

How would you like to be the doctor who had to pull the plug when the courts in New Jersey ruled that Karen Ann Quinlan need no longer be kept alive by a respirator? Or suppose you were three-year-old Chad Green's doctor in Massachusetts and knew that you could keep him alive by chemotherapy but had to go to court to convince his parents that this was the proper treatment. What would you do? You're an obstetrician and you've just delivered a baby so badly deformed that the medical bills just to keep him or her alive will keep the family in debt for years. Will you let the baby die though it is your job to preserve life? How about the doctor who is keeping someone alive on a respirator though he or she has been in a coma for three months and cannot possibly function normally again, while another patient is waiting for a kidney? What should that doctor do?

These days physicians and the rest of society must struggle with ethical and moral problems that did not exist before. Technological advances and a new questioning attitude on the part of many patients have forced doctors as well as other people to change their attitudes.

A study done in 1961 revealed that 80 percent of doctors did not tell their patients they were going to die, although 80 percent of people surveyed said they wanted to know. A recent report in the *Journal of the American Medical Association* claims that most doctors now tell their patients they are dying. According to Sissela Bok, who teaches medical ethics at Harvard Medical School, "Truthful information humanely conveyed, helps patients cope with illness, helps them tolerate pain better, need less medication and even recover faster after surgery." * Lying to them deprives them of the right to decide how to spend their remaining days or weeks.

Why don't doctors always tell patients the truth?

"Because I don't want to admit to myself that a patient is dying," said one doctor. A neurologist who specializes in brain tumors, he does not want to rob his patient of hope. "If a patient doesn't want to face the thought of death, I cannot be the one to tell him."

Dr. Kubler-Ross, who has talked to hundreds of dying people and has reached an understanding of the way they wish to be treated by doctors, always counsels medical students to be honest, but never to take away hope. "The question should not be, 'Should we

* Sissela Bok. "The Doctor's Dilemma." *New York Times,* April 18, 1978.

tell?' " she says. "But rather, 'How do I share this with my patient?' "

"If a doctor can speak freely with his patients about the diagnosis of malignancy without equating it necessarily with death, he will do the patient a great service. He should at the same time leave the door open for hope, namely, new drugs, treatments, chances of new techniques and new research. That it is a battle they are going to fight together—patient, family, and doctor. All the patients know about their terminal illness anyway, whether they were told or not, but they depend greatly on the physician to present the news in an acceptable manner." *

Dr. Dennis Allendorf, Assistant Director of Pediatrics at St. Luke's Hospital in New York, thinks it is especially important to tell teenagers they are dying. "Everybody has a right to know as much about his or her life as possible. It's especially important for a teenager to know what's going on with his or her body. This is the age for exploring, experimentation, trying to find out some of the answers to life. I've spent many hours talking to parents to convince them the child should know. They feel it is their duty as parents to shield the child from harmful knowledge. But once they realize the child really has a right to know and tell him or her, that child changes from a rather

* Elisabeth Kubler-Ross. *On Death and Dying.* New York: Macmillan Publishing Company, Inc., 1969, p. 28ff.

recalcitrant patient into someone who is anxious to help with the therapy. Then we can level with the child, and answer questions honestly. A few weeks ago, one of my patients was dying of leukemia but his parents refused to tell him. When he did die, the parents were cleaning out his desk and they found thirty magazine articles on leukemia. He knew."

When I asked high school juniors whether they would want to know if they were going to die, most said yes at first, and then, upon reflection, qualified that answer.

"I think you have a right to know you're going to die," one girl said. "You'd want to make a will and say goodbye to people you love. You'd want to make arrangements for your funeral."

"It's easy to say you want to know when you're dying," said another student. "But when you really think about someone telling you you're going to die, that's scary. I don't know if I'd be strong enough to handle it."

"There are people I wouldn't want to tell me the time, much less the fact that I was dying," another boy said. "They should teach medical students how to talk to dying patients."

Because of courses on handling death and dying in medical schools, and workshops and seminars all over the country for nurses, social workers, chaplains, and other members of the helping professions, the attitude toward the dying patient is gradually changing. There were 120,000 conferences on death and dying in 1977. Dr. Mwalimu Imara, director of the Boston Center of Religion and Psychotherapy, emphasizes the importance of doctors and nurses learning to deal with grief. "The dying patient who cannot talk about it, suffers grief, the family is subjected to severe grief, but doctors and nurses working with patients accumulate many smaller griefs that build over a period of time." *

We know now that a dying patient needs the kindness and caring of everyone concerned—staff and family—the sort of kindness that can let the person go knowing he or she is loved and cherished by friends and relatives. More nurses are trained to recognize the five stages of dying and grieving so they can understand that the anger or depression of a terminally ill person is a normal reaction. More doctors are trying to include patients in discussions of their care.

One of the most difficult ethical, moral, and legal problems facing society today is whether to keep a patient alive with extraordinary means when there is very little hope that he or she will ever function normally again. This dilemma was dramatized in 1976 when the parents of Karen Ann Quinlan won permission from the New Jersey Supreme Court to

---

* Claire Huff. "Medical Care For the Terminally Ill: A Group Here Expresses Its Concern." *The Inquirer*, November 5, 1978, p. 4.

disconnect the respirator that had been keeping Karen alive for a year in a coma. The court ruling states that the guardian of a patient in a coma could decide whether to disconnect the respirator and other life-support systems when "there is no reasonable possibility they will ever recover to a cognitive, sapient state."

Because Karen's doctors believe that Karen's brain will never regain the functions it has lost, they slowly weaned her from the respirator. Now, three years later and still in a coma, she breathes without the aid of the respirator in a New Jersey nursing home.

Even more recently, in February 1979, a judge in Los Angeles ruled that a respirator could be disconnected in the case of a three-year-old boy whose brain damage was pronounced irreversible by doctors. This was the first decision in which the patient was a minor, and unusual because the courts usually decide in favor of saving a child's life. In this instance, Judge Richard Byrne said, "Where there is no possibility of recovery, the interests of the state in compelling treatment are outweighed by the individual's right to privacy." * The judge left the decision of when to disconnect the respirator up to the parents.

In most cases, decisions like this one never reach the courts. Respirators are often turned off when it is obvious that the patient will die. In order to decide when extraordinary means should be used to keep a

* *New York Times*, February 18, 1979.

patient breathing, new guidelines are being formed to define death.

In most states, a patient is considered still alive if his or her heart is beating and he or she is breathing, even if machines are keeping those functions going. Some states now have laws redefining death as the condition when the brain completely loses its functions and can never regain them. In 1968 a Harvard ad hoc committee drew up new criteria for measuring irreversible coma which include: No response, no movements or breathing, and no reflexes. In addition, a flat electroencephalogram is used for confirmation. These tests are not valid in cases of drug poisoning and lowered body temperatures. The tests are repeated after 24 hours.

There are legal problems that arise when there is no clear-cut definition of death. In cases of assault leading to complete loss of brain function, defense lawyers have already tried to prove that the doctors were the real murderers. They claim the victim died not as a result of the bullet wound in the head inflicted by their client, but because the respirator was turned off in the hospital, killing the patient. The opposition maintains that the patient was already dead when brain function ceased. It becomes important in cases where a husband and wife, each with a different heir, are in an automobile accident together. The wife is dead and the husband is being kept alive on a respirator although his brain no longer functions. Was he dead when his heart stopped after the respirator was turned off, or when his brain died during the accident? The courts must decide whether the husband or wife died last to determine who the heir should be.

Aside from legal questions, however, society faces difficult moral dilemmas in the practice of medicine. Should a severely deformed baby be kept alive by extraordinary means? If it seems likely that a baby would probably die in a short time anyway, or if doctors knew that life for the child and the parents would be unbearably difficult if the child were helped to survive, the baby is often allowed to die. That is, he or she is fed and changed and kept in a warm room, but no surgery or extraordinary life-prolonging means are used.

Relatives and others must also face the serious and difficult moral issue of whether to pull the plug of a respirator if a patient is suffering or if there is irreversible brain damage. The teenagers I talked to felt strongly about this.

"I would not want to be kept alive by a machine if I would just be a vegetable when I came out of a coma," said one high school senior in Ohio. "There should be a state law respecting my right to die."

Eight states have now passed Right to Die laws (also called Natural Death Acts or Living Will Acts): California, Idaho, Oregon, New Mexico, Nevada, Texas, North Carolina, and Arkansas. Legislation is being considered in the other 42 states. The laws must be written very carefully so they cannot be interpreted as permitting mercy killings, and as a result they are too cautiously worded to help most people. Most of them are modeled on the California law, The Natural Death Act, which is only binding if the patient has been certified as terminally ill at least fourteen days before the will is signed. California's law does not cover victims of stroke or accidents, unless they are so certified, nor does it cover a terminally ill child or a pregnant woman. The other states passed modified versions of this law. Some people feel such bills interfere with the doctor's right to make decisions about his or her patients. Dennis J. Horan, a partner in a Chicago law firm, writing in the American Bar Association publication, *The Forum*, says, "The California bill adds officious burdens to the death bed, encumbers medical decisions with unnecessary additional consultations and creates rather than clarifies legal problems." *

Indeed, Mr. Horan feels that in order to protect himself from malpractice suits, a doctor will use extraordinary means to keep a patient alive unless the person has written a Living Will. Without a Right to Die law, the doctor uses his or her own judgment and often turns off the respirator when it is known to be useless.

People continue to write Living Wills, requesting the right to die with dignity, though they may not be legally binding, because it is a more permanent expression of their wishes than a spoken desire. In 1973,

---

* Dennis J. Horan. "The 'Right to Die' Legislative and Judicial Developments." *The Forum*, Winter, 1978.

the American Medical Association passed a "Death with Dignity" resolution which supports patients' decisions to stop treatment.

It is often impossible for doctors to predict the exact extent of brain damage that will occur after a coma. There was a brilliant physicist who was in a coma for two months after an accident with no pulse, no blood pressure, and a flat EEG. When he regained consciousness, he was deaf, blind, without reflexes, and couldn't speak. Doctors fought to bring him back, and eleven months later he sat up in bed and accepted the Nobel Prize. He lived for six years after that.*

Just recently a young man in Chicago was injured in an accident and lay in a coma for two-and-a-half months. His fiancée refused to believe that he would never move or speak again. She sat by his bed every day encouraging him to fight. With her love and energy, and the help of occupational therapists at the hospital, he regained his ability to walk, speak, and swim, and they were married two years later. His rehabilitation continues, but he's an example of why doctors don't give up easily.

Recovery depends on whether oxygen is still going to the brain while the patient is in a coma. Tests can determine the amount of oxygen the brain is receiving, and even if there is a flat EEG, if there is enough oxygen, the brain does not die. In cases of

* David Dempsey. *The Way We Die*. New York: Macmillan Publishing Co., Inc., 1975, p. 21.

overdoses of drugs or hypothermia (very low body temperature), there is always a flat EEG, and people can still recover.

The young people I interviewed rejected the idea of living for months or years in a coma, hooked up to a machine that kept the heart beating after the brain had lost its ability to function.

"Think of all those people who could use your kidneys," Bill, a senior said. "They could be living useful lives while you lie there waiting to die."

There are 45,000 people with kidney ailments in the United States and Medicare is increasingly reluctant to pick up the $900 million needed to pay for dialysis treatments. There are only 800 treatment centers available. It is obvious that kidney transplants are the only answer for these people, but there is a shortage of donors. Add one more dilemma to society's already burdened shoulders: Should a doctor pull the plug of someone being kept alive on a respirator, though the brain no longer functions, to use the kidney for a young person whose kidneys are failing?

With hospital costs increasing 15 percent every year and some hospital rooms as high as $300 a day, a family could easily be impoverished by a hospital stay beyond the length of time paid for by hospitalization insurance.

The courts and concerned members of our society are reluctant to permit pulling the plug because they are afraid the next step would be permission to commit "mercy killings." Many people believe that letting someone die without prolonging his or her life with artificial means is a different thing entirely from actually taking steps to end that life.

In *Jean's Way*, a book written to advocate changing the laws which now prohibit mercy killings, Englishman Derek Humphrey tells of the pact he made with his wife who was dying of cancer. According to their plan, he would put poison in her coffee before the pain became unbearable. There have been other mercy killings too, such as the boy who shot his brother, paralyzed in an accident, and the father who drowned his retarded son. The courts have never accepted mercy as a defense, but have usually been lenient in such cases.

And if society doesn't have enough dilemmas to solve, there is a new one facing it—whether to use marijuana to alleviate the symptoms of chemotherapy. Ted Rosenthal discovered the beneficial effects of pot while he was being treated for leukemia: "The drug I've been on for the last couple of weeks causes acute nausea that no drug, no pill will do anything to help. My doctor came rushing in one day and said, 'Do you have any access to weed?' And I said, 'What kind of weed do you mean?' And he said, 'Weed, grass, marijuana.' So I got some that night, and I decided to wait until I was at my worst. I sat there with a bowl in my lap ready to vomit and a pipe of pot in my other hand, and just as I was about to let loose, I took a puff, and whee, it was gone. I felt fine. And I went right in after two or three puffs and ate a dozen clams and a huge lobster and a piece of chocolate cake. I went rushing back to the doctor and told him, and he said, 'Fantastic!' So he's got me on pot now." *

There is evidence that marijuana may also be helpful in treating epilepsy, alcoholism, multiple sclerosis, and in preventing blindness and helping asthmatics. Only four states have laws that allow the use of marijuana in research programs: New Mexico, Florida, Louisiana, and Illinois. A doctor practicing in a state without such a law might suggest to a cancer patient that marijuana could relieve the nausea which is a side effect of chemotherapy, but he or she can't prescribe or supply it. Therefore, since it is illegal the patient would have to find his own—not too difficult a task today, it seems, when 11 million Americans seem to find a regular supply everywhere from high schools to the White House. One man was arrested for growing marijuana which he needed to save his eyesight. Only after a court battle in which he proved that only pot could prevent his blindness was he allowed to use it. The National Organization for the Reform of Marijuana Laws has been active in trying to persuade the Food and Drug Administration to consider the medical and therapeutic uses of the drug.

A new questioning attitude on the part of patients has sometimes resulted in the rejection of a course of treatment suggested by a doctor. Although adults have always had the right to refuse treatment

---

* Ted Rosenthal. *How Could I Not Be Among You."* (*Film*).

for religious or other reasons, courts have been less clear in deciding treatment for a child.

How far should parents go in deciding what is in the best interest of their children? Dr. Dennis Allendorf, Assistant Director of Pediatrics at St. Luke's Hospital in New York, says, "The doctor has his own moral obligation to do what he thinks is best for the child. When parents go to a professional with a problem, they have done their duty as a parent, and the kind of therapy used is the doctor's obligation. The parents are not expert in this area and should trust the doctor's opinion as to the proper therapy to be used. I certainly listen to parents, however, and if they feel strongly about something, we can usually reach a compromise. After all, both the parents and the doctor want what's best for the child. I recently had a child with a tumor of the eye. We recommended three types of therapy: surgery, chemotherapy, and radiation. The parents did not want to have chemotherapy but would allow radiation and surgery. We reviewed all the studies we could find, and found that in most tumors of this kind, the chances of survival with chemotherapy were at most 1 percent increased. The child was cured with radiation and surgery. If they had refused all treatment, then I think we'd have had to go to court to gain the rights of the child."

One of the most difficult problems facing society as a whole is the question of abortion. In 1973 the Supreme Court ruled that a woman has the right to choose an abortion if she doesn't wish to complete a pregnancy. Laws preventing that right were declared unconstitutional. During the time that abortion was illegal, women were forced to go to unscrupulous people who performed this simple operation, usually without anesthetic or sterile instruments. Many women died, some became sterile. Since the Supreme Court decision, women who do not wish to have a child—and can afford an abortion—can end a pregnancy safely, with very little discomfort, and often with counseling to help avoid an unwanted pregnancy in the future.

The Catholic Church condemns abortion, as do the Mormon Church and fundamentalist sects in the South, as well as Orthodox Jews. Other Protestant denominations and reform Jews consider abortion a matter of choice, to be decided by each woman according to her own conscience.

Anti-abortionists are conservative, sincerely motivated people who believe abortion is morally wrong. They have formed strong lobbying groups to promote a constitutional amendment which would make abortions illegal again.

Some doctors on hospital staffs may refuse to perform abortions, and many do so because of their own ethical or religious beliefs, but safe, inexpensive abortion clinics are readily available today. Pro-choice advocates believe the state should not be placed in the position of deciding which set of beliefs should dominate our society.

CHAPTER V
SUICIDE

Sandy killed herself when she was seventeen. Everyone said, "She was such a nice, quiet girl. I didn't know her very well, but she didn't seem like the kind who would commit suicide." Sandy's father was an engineer who traveled a great deal. Her mother worried about the cost of educating four children. She didn't understand why Sandy spent so much time in her room, why she slept so much, why she didn't seem to have any friends. She scolded Sandy about her grades. One of Sandy's few friends said, "She asked me what would happen if she took a whole bottle of Valium. I didn't think she was serious."

Bob shot himself when he was nineteen. That was his seventh unsuccessful attempt at suicide in three years. His mother married five times and put her son in a series of foster homes when she was unable to care for him herself. When she was able to have him at home, he was often beaten by one or another of his stepfathers. Bob's real father was an alcoholic who left his mother when Bob was born. His mother often told him, "You're a bum just like your father." Bob drank and took drugs from early adolescence on. He married at eighteen, but was divorced by the time he was nineteen, without ever seeing his own child.

The number of suicides among people fifteen to twenty-four is increasing every year. It is the second cause of death, after accidents, in this age group. The suicide rate among children ten to fourteen is rising too. Almost 5,000 young people committed suicide in 1975, and that number includes only those deaths reported as suicides. Many so-called accidents are actually suicides, but aren't reported as such because of the stigma attached. The number of attempted suicides is seven times higher. Nobody can estimate how many people kill themselves slowly with alcohol, or by overeating, smoking, or taking drugs.

Only white men between the ages of seventy and seventy-four have a higher rate of suicide than adolescents, although recently women in the forty-five to forty-nine age group have been catching up. Doctors, especially psychiatrists, are the most likely candidates, with dentists and military officers not far behind. More people kill themselves during holidays than at any other time of the year, and late spring and early summer are the most popular seasons for suicide.

According to statistics, girls attempt suicide more often than boys, but boys succeed more often. One reason for this is because girls usually choose pills and wrist slashing, while boys tend to use guns or hang themselves. There is a new form of self-destructive behavior among young girls, called anorexia nervosa, a form of self-imposed starvation. Often they must be hospitalized to keep them alive.

Why are so many young people desperate enough to take their own lives? Jim Jerome, writing in the *New York Times Magazine,* January 4, 1979, about the increase in suicide among children between ten and fourteen, suggests there is a "deeply ingrained mythology of childhood as a period of carefree discovery, innocence and fantasy." He cites a failure among psychiatrists to diagnose depression in children because they have considered it to be an adult disorder. The high rate of divorce in this country—more than one million in 1976—can, in some cases, lead to depression and suicide, although there are other factors involved. "Rage felt toward the absent love object often provokes feelings of guilt, since the child may feel responsible for the death of the failed marriage. This intolerable guilt then triggers a reaction of self-hatred." *

"I think it's very easy to understand why teenagers commit suicide," Dr. Allendorf says. "Their ego strengths begin to emerge for the first time when they're going through puberty. Their first rejection and acceptance by the opposite sex occurs then. There are pressures on them to become productive members of society. They must do something creative on their own, instead of just memorizing facts. They begin to realize their parents are imperfect. They can

* Jim Jerome. "Catching Them Before Suicide." *The New York Times Magazine.* January 14, 1979, p. 31.

be crushed so easily, rejected so easily by their peer groups or other people they respect. It's a very tender age."

When I asked students in high school and college why they thought the suicide rate was so high among their age group, this is what they told me:

"There's a lot of pressure from parents and teachers about what you're going to do after high school," said one senior. "Which college, what major, which graduate school. You may know what you want to do but don't know how to go about doing it."

"There's even more pressure on college students," said a college freshman, "Especially in the Ivy League colleges, where a lot of them are trying to get into law school or medical school." Northwestern University accepted 110 medical students out of 7500 applicants in 1977. In an examination of suicide on college campuses, shown on a television documentary called "College Can Be Killing," the impersonality of large college communities was one factor that led to feelings of isolation and hopelessness. One freshman tried to kill himself by taking pills and alcohol. He threw up, slept it off, and went back to class. No one had even missed him. Pressure to justify the enormous amount of money it costs to go to college these days leads many students to the point of attempted suicide.

"Kids our age are looking for something," said a high school sophomore. "It's the age when you try to reach out for something. You need a lot of friendships, a lot of relationships in your life. Many of us just can't find that."

"A lot of kids get depressed when they have problems with their parents," said another teenager. "They're afraid to talk about their problems and keep them bottled up inside because they don't think their parents will understand. Parents look back and say, 'These are the best years of your life. How come you're having such a rough time? Don't get so upset by your adolescence. Enjoy it because you're never going to go through it again.' Who wants to go through it again?"

"There are so many divorces now," said another student. "Sometimes teenagers think they did something to cause the divorce. We tend to blame ourselves for everything."

One bizarre cause of the increase in suicides among young people is a belief in reincarnation, according to Dr. William Worden of the Harvard Medical School. Dr. Worden is doing research on suicide at the Suicide Prevention Clinic at Massachusetts General Hospital in Boston. He found that some young people really believe they will be born again and do not consider death an end to life.

One college freshman said to me, "I'm kind of looking forward to death, just to try something new. It's another place to go. I'm really curious to find out what's on the other side." Later his professor told me that he had attempted suicide twice.

Why does one person commit suicide, while another, subjected to the same background, environment, upbringing, pressures, and other factors cited by psychologists, does not? There are enough theories, many of them conflicting, to confuse anyone struggling to understand how a person could take his or her life. Some say it is definitely explained by the way a child is reared: either too dependent on the mother, thus feeling guilty every time he or she broke off a relationship; or too independent, with no feeling of belonging, of roots, or a place in the world, thus becoming alienated.

Perhaps it can be explained by geography, say others. The introverted Northern races in Scandinavia, Germany, and England are more apt to commit suicide than the explosive extroverts in Mediterranean countries like Italy and Greece. The highest rate of suicide in the world is in West Germany.

You could blame it on long, dark, dreary winters, or on the new moon. Some think hormonal changes during adolescence or menopause are responsible for higher suicide rates at those times. There's a theory that suicides are contagious, especially among young people and that the suicide of one person suggests a similar solution to others. That seemed to be the opinion recently in Ridgewood, New Jersey, where two boys killed themselves and one attempted suicide. There was certainly no common factor that could be held up as a reason for the suicides. One boy was popular, athletic, successful with his peers and adults and came from a close, loving family. The other, also from a loving family, though his mother had divorced and remarried, was a loner, isolated, with few friends, already labeled a "boy with suicidal tendencies" by the school psychologist. Other wealthy suburban communities, such as Chappaqua, in New York's Westchester County, had an increase in adolescent suicides recently. Why? No one seems to know, and there certainly is no similar pattern in the backgrounds of these teenagers.

There are more suicides in Oriental societies than in the West—particularly in Japan, where killing oneself is considered an honorable kind of death. Christians and Muslims, who are forbidden to escape through suicide, have a lower rate.

There are enough psychological theories on suicide to satisfy anyone. The most famous one is Emile Durkheim's theory of anomie, a state of anxiety and isolation produced by living in a society which no longer sets standards of behavior. When there is a change in a person's life, whether a good change like marriage or a promotion, or a change for the worse, like a death or divorce, the stress caused can precipitate suicide. Durkheim, writing in 1897, also classified suicides into egoistic, altruistic, and fatalistic. Egoistic suicide is caused by feelings of alienation and isolation from the rest of society, a common modern malady. Altruistic suicide is a death for idealistic reasons —heroic deaths in wars, for instance. Fatalistic suicides occur when a person feels he or she has no hope of escaping a situation—prison, for example.

Psychoanalyst Alfred Adler blamed the child-parent relationship which produces an adult with an inferiority complex, while his colleague Karl Menninger says that a suicide contains within himself or herself the wish to kill, the wish to be killed, and the wish to die. Freud believed we all carry a death instinct within us that is always in conflict with our instinct of self-preservation.

No one theory explains why some people commit suicide and others don't. Sociologists blame forces in society, while psychologists look for flaws in the individual. Robert Kastenbaum and Ruth Aisenberg suggest that factors such as a poor grade in an exam, breaking up with a boyfriend or girlfriend, or a rainy Monday may precipitate a suicide, but that the real, underlying causes can be traced to emotional scars incurred during childhood.*

But whatever the precipitating, immediate reason may be, people commit suicide because they find life too painful to continue. They may hope somone will stop them, but they are desperate enough to take their own lives because they see no solution to their problems.

Dr. Calvin Frederick, president of the American Association of Suicidology, founded in 1968, suggests warning signals that should be taken seriously by friends and parents of potential suicide victims:

---

* Robert Kastenbaum and Ruth Aisenberg. *The Psychology of Death*. New York: Springer Publishing Co., Inc., 1972, p. 251ff.

1. A marked change in behavior
2. Loss of appetite
3. Erratic sleep habits
4. Giving away a prized possession
5. Staying isolated behind a locked door
6. Verbal clues, such as, "I wish
    I never had to wake up again."
7. Red eyes and dilated pupils

Dr. Frederick looks for a pattern of "haplessness, helplessness, and hopelessness." The typical young male suicide, he says, has a very poor relationship with his father, and his father usually has left home. The boy feels rejected and has a poor self-image. He usually smokes heavily, drinks, and takes drugs.

According to Dr. Frederick, the female suicide often has a self-centered, narcissistic mother who makes neurotic demands on her daughter, and her father is weak and ineffectual. She therefore turns to a boyfriend who cannot solve her problems and rejects her. Both male and female adolescents who attempt or succeed in suicide are usually brighter than average, and are more confused by the complex world that exists today and have more difficulty finding their own place in that world.

There are more than 200 suicide prevention centers connected with hospitals and universities in this country, as well as telephone hot lines set up to help troubled young people realize there are other alternatives to taking their own lives.

Dr. Coralee Levine-Schneidman, a clinical psychologist, supervised graduate students at a crisis intervention clinic at Yeshiva University in New York. The name was changed from suicide clinic because "People get very frightened at the word *suicide*. They feel if they go to a suicide clinic, they will be considered strange or crazy, whereas a crisis intervention center sounds less threatening."

The clinic was advertised in local TV spots which announced, "If you have a problem, a sudden crisis, or you're depressed, or if you're thinking of suicide, call this number." People came in to the center as they would to a hospital emergency room. The job of the counselors was to help these people understand that there are other options open to them besides suicide.

"Suicide patients see no options," says Dr. Levine-Schneidman. "They feel trapped. Our job is to find out what prompted the suicide thought—what the trap is. We get very quickly to that part of it. We don't do long-term treatment. If there is a need for that, the patient is sent to another clinic. If you are thinking of suicide and feel you have no choice, the minute another person understands it the trap begins to open, you're not so closed in.

"Also, people who seek out a crisis intervention clinic or call a hot line are a special group of people. Those who seek help are saying something—there's a strong part of them that does not want to use this approach. By even spelling out what the trap is, a person can see a way out. Even if the possibilities are not workable, the patient begins to think in terms of options rather than of being trapped, with only one solution—suicide."

The main lesson to be learned in studying suicide is that there are ways to prevent it, and that, in many cases, the despair that causes a person to want to die is only temporary. Most people want to be stopped. If someone you know talks even half-seriously about taking pills or jumping out the window, it's important to get help for that person immediately. Don't say, "Oh, don't be silly, you know you don't mean that." Tell the person you understand the way he or she feels and persuade them to talk to somebody on a telephone hot line, or a crisis intervention center, or a counseling center at a university. Don't take a chance.

CHAPTER VI
BURIAL OR CREMATION

Come with me on a tour of a typical American funeral home. The grounds are as carefully tended as they must be in heaven. Green lawns and ivy borders soothe the eye and calm one's fears. Inside the dignified mansion, the pale green walls and silken drapes are even more reassuring. The director, never smiling too much, gently guides you into the thickly-carpeted, softly-lit room where grieving relatives come to plan the details of the funeral and to be comforted.

In another room more brightly lit are caskets as simple as the $70 plywood job and as elaborate as the bronze, velvet-lined beauty which costs $3,500. Your own conscience, the amount of guilt you feel toward your loved one, plus a little nudging from the mortician, will probably tempt you to spend more than you planned. If the Federal Trade Commission has its way, it will soon be illegal for him to press you to spend more than you want to. New regulations affecting the $4 billion funeral industry in this country are presently being considered and if they are adopted,

the following restrictions will be imposed on the ve-
hemently-protesting funeral directors:

1.   No embalming will be done without permission from the family. Although some undertakers will
tell you that embalming is required by law, it is not
required in any state unless the body is to be transported to another place.
2.   An itemized bill would be required instead of the
all-inclusive figure now presented without explanation
to surviving relatives. Funerals can cost $2,000 or
$3,000 and many feel some of the services included
in that figure are not necessary.
3.   Inexpensive caskets will have to be displayed as
well as the expensive ones. Funeral directors would
be prohibited from using pressure on customers to
buy a costly model.
4.   Morticians must present a printed price list on
request and these prices must be quoted on the phone.
5.   No interference will be allowed in arrangements
between other businesses and one of the non-profit
memorial societies which provide simple, inexpensive
burials and cremations for their members. In other
words, an undertaker might threaten to discontinue
business with a limousine service that also provides
cars to memorial societies. That would no longer be
allowed.

It was Jessica Mitford's *The American Way of Death*,
and Ruth Mulveyn Harmer's *The High Cost of Dying*,

both published in 1963, which were responsible for clamping down on the funeral industry. Ms. Mitford, in her wildly funny book, accused the industry of taking advantage of people too grief-stricken to think clearly, and of profiting from their sorrow. She pointed out the grotesque incongruity of offering a choice of either a foam rubber or innerspring mattress for the coffin, of providing special shoes to fit the rigor mortised feet of the corpse, and she especially objected to the unnecessary embalming practiced by most undertakers. Consumer groups have been urging government regulation of morticians for years, but the 14,000-member National Funeral Directors Association has lobbied vigorously against any kind of control.

The services of the funeral director might run from $400 to $800, depending on where you live, and usually include visiting the hospital, obtaining the death certificate, preparing the body for burial or cremation, sending obituaries or notices to the newspapers, phoning relatives and friends, making arrangements for the viewing, the funeral service, and the burial or cremation. Some morticians even help widows with taxes and financial problems after the death of their husbands.

To prepare for their vocation, funeral directors attend mortuary school for two years, where they might study psychology, sociology, accounting, management, and mortuary law, as well as embalming. After a period of apprenticeship, they take state boards and are then licensed to work in the funeral business. Recently, some morticians have taken special courses in eye enucleation for cornea transplants.

Funeral directors, beset by hostility on all sides, have tried to counteract their mercenary image by emphasizing their counseling services for the bereaved. "We are often the only ones who listen," said one. "We encourage people to talk about the person who has died. We also follow up our original work with a phone call about a month later to find out if there is anything we can do to help. Most people want to talk about their problems even if there really isn't anything anyone can do. We listen."

In addition, many funeral directors offer slide presentations and tours of their establishments to high school classes, and most young people seem to find these trips informative and useful in dispelling their fears about dead bodies and the mysterious rites they imagined took place in the basements of funeral homes.

"Its a good thing to learn about the practical details of a funeral," one high school junior said. "If you know ahead of time whether a person wants a $70 coffin or a $3,000 one, whether he or she wants to be cremated or buried, or what kind of a service he or she wants, you can just concentrate on remembering the person."

"They showed us the room where they prepare the bodies," one girl said. "It's just a clean room with two slanted tables in it, where they put the bodies to take the blood out. There was nothing horrible about it at all."

"We saw a $3,500 mahogany, hand-made African casket that was lined in cardboard!" one boy said indignantly. "You'd think they could put a better lining in it for $3,500."

"The expensive caskets were watertight and airtight and had a thirty-year warranty," said a discerning senior. "Who's going to check after thirty years to see if any water got in. The corpse wouldn't care anyway."

Elaborate, expensive funerals were definitely not the way to go for most of the young people I talked to. One young girl expressed the opinion of most of her classmates when she said, "I don't think it's necessary to have an elaborate casket and an expensive funeral. Why can't you just be wrapped in a cloth and buried? When you die, you enrich the earth as your body decomposes. It's unnatural to put someone in a corrosion-proof coffin. And on top of the price of the coffin, you have to pay for a vault to keep the earth from collapsing onto the casket. They cost $200 or $300 more. Big funerals just make undertakers richer and families poorer."

Some kind of ritual is an important part of the grieving process, say psychologists, and each religion has its own rites and ceremonies for easing the pain of death.

Cremation is forbidden to Orthodox Jews, who

bury their dead within twenty-four hours. Autopsies are normally not allowed, nor can there be any metal in the coffin. There is a mourning period of seven days, called sitting shivah, in which those who hold strictly to Jewish laws do not cook, read, or even look in a mirror. A piece of clothing is torn to symbolize grief. It is a time when relatives and friends visit the bereaved and talk about the deceased. Lisa, a college freshman who is Jewish, thinks this is an excellent way to deal with grief.

"It's very therapeutic," she says. "Instead of avoiding the topic and discussing other subjects, the dead person is talked about and praised. During the seven days, the family begins to get used to the person's death and can then continue their own lives. It gives them some time to adjust to the shock of the death before going back to everyday life."

Catholics are more apt to bury their dead than cremate them, although cremation has not been forbidden by the Church since 1963. The burial usually takes place three days after the death. Relatives and friends visit the funeral home where the casket can be either open or closed. The casket is not usually open at the funeral service in the church. After a requiem mass in which the congregation may participate in responsive readings, the body is transported to the grave, and there is another ceremony there.

Elaine, who comes from a large, traditional, Italian family, explains her feelings about the Catholic wake and funeral: "We celebrate death in our family. We believe you go to a better life in heaven, so it's a time for celebration. We all get together and cry, but not because we don't accept it. We're sad to lose the person who died, but happy for him because God took him to a better life. I think funerals are necessary."

Another boy with a Catholic background, Kevin, had strong feelings about viewing the body. "I just can't see looking at a dead body," he said. "To see people lying in a box, all prepared, with their hair neatly combed and eyes closed is terrible. I don't want my friends and family looking down on me like a dressed-up doll, saying, 'He didn't look like that in real life.' "

"I think viewing the body is necessary in order to accept the person's death," Elaine answered. "I don't want to stare at a closed box."

"When I die," Bill said, "I want a full Catholic mass on the beach at Cape Cod at sunrise with all my family and friends there."

Protestants, too, may choose either cremation or burial. Some prefer open coffins, but the Episcopalians insist on a closed casket. There is usually a visitation at the funeral home, a church service, often with a eulogy praising the deceased, and a ceremony at the grave. Unitarians usually prefer cremation with a memorial service. Quakers stress simplicity and some dig the grave themselves.

There is often a flexibility and individuality in Protestant funerals. Many families vary the traditional ceremony in accordance with the last wishes of the deceased. Jenny is a high school senior in Connecticut who remembers her grandmother's funeral with affection.

"My grandmother didn't want a long drawn-out funeral with sad music, so we sang some of her favorite hymns. My mother wrote a eulogy about her mother and read it at the funeral. My grandmother suffered so much before she died, that it was a good thing it happened. It wasn't really sad."

Funeral customs in other lands and cultures are as varied as the people who invented them. Everyone knows the ancient Egyptians had the most elaborate burial customs with the most efficient methods of preserving the bodies that have ever been devised. When unwrapped 3,000 years later, the skin on the soles of the feet of some of the corpses was still soft and pliable. By removing the viscera and filling the body cavities with herbs and wrapping cloth carefully around the dead person, the Egyptians achieved almost perfect preservation. This was very important to them because they believed a person's soul, called Ka, lived on after death, but could not exist without the presence of the body. To ease life in the Egyptian heaven, furniture, clothing, jewelry, and other personal possessions were buried in the tomb for use by the soul. Since the Egyptians believed the soul must do some useful work in the afterlife, such as tilling the soil, they often included small statues in the tomb to do the work. The soul, Ka, had to be judged by Osiris,

King of the Dead, so a Book of the Dead, sort of an etiquette book for the dead, was also placed in the tomb. Egyptian coffins were made of stone, wood, papier-mâché, glass, or earthenware.

The materials used for coffins throughout the ages were, of course, determined by what was available in the area. The American Indians used canoes or baskets as coffins, or wrapped the dead either in blankets or buffalo robes. In Australia, the aborigines use bark or wicker to form coffins. There have been coffins made of large stones, tree trunks, burnt clay, lead, and iron.

Primitive tribes in Australia believe the soul stays near the body after death, and the ghosts must be propitiated with gifts of food and clothing. Funeral rites and customs are strictly followed, for it is believed that the person's soul hovers nearby to watch the ceremony. So great is the fear of the ghost among some Australian tribes that the village is burned down after a burial and the people move to a new location. Mourners must not say the name of the dead person aloud lest the ghost become angry.

Polynesians believe death is caused by an angry god. Sickness is looked upon as punishment for an evil act, and very little is done in the way of treatment besides some exorcism by the medicine man. Lest you think this is an ignorant point of view, you might recall that Christian Scientists also believe sickness is due to incorrect thinking and that reading by the bedside of the one in error will heal the patient.

Cremation was a common method of disposing

of bodies in ancient times. The funeral pyre was accepted by many societies. The Christian belief in resurrection of the body often led to burial instead, and that view still prevails among many Christians. However, in the interest of saving space and an increasing belief that there is no life after death, cremation is becoming more popular in this country. Even so, only 5 percent of the population now choose this form of disposal of the body, usually those who live in large cities or in Florida or California where there are large elderly populations and space for burial is limited. We haven't really promoted the idea of cremation here as they have in more crowded countries, such as Japan, where 75 percent of all bodies are cremated, or in England, where 60 percent of the dead are cremated, and also in Scandinavia, where cremation is popular.

I visited a crematorium outside Philadelphia with a high school class and was surprised to find it such a pleasant place. This one was a lovely old stone chapel covered with ivy, at the top of a hill overlooking green lawns and shady walks. The small chapel inside was softly lit, carpeted with oriental rugs and banked with green plants on both sides of the simple, lighted cross in the center. The cross could be replaced by a Star of David when the deceased was Jewish.

In rooms called sanctuaries, urns of different shapes and metals stood behind glass windows or were concealed behind stone blocks. The price depended on the size of the niche, whether the urn was placed behind glass or stone, what kind of material surrounded the glass niches, and whether or not they were at eye level. Those lower or higher cost less. In one sanctuary there was a magnificent grandfather's clock that had been willed to the crematorium by a lady in a nearby urn. In her will, she provided a fund to maintain the clock in good condition.

Prices of the urns ranged from $40 for a light-weight steel urn to over $600 for a large, cast bronze model. The niches cost from around $135 to $600 for a large glass-fronted case. Urns can also be buried outside in special gardens for that purpose. Scattering the remains of a loved one in your own garden at home or on a favorite vacation spot is discouraged by most crematorium managers. Our guide warned us that some states restrict the scattering of cremated remains, or "cremains" (he never used the word *ashes*). He told us about one man who put his wife's remains in the trunk of his car, but he never had the courage to take them out and scatter them in her rose garden as she had requested. A year later he returned to have the ashes put in an urn and buried in the garden at the crematorium. They had remained in his car all that time. I did have the feeling that strewing ashes was frowned on because it meant far less money to the crematorium, which could charge for the urn, the niche or garden spot, and the maintenance.

In most places it costs between $70 and $200 to be cremated. That includes the use of the chapel, the service, and the cremation. Usually the body must be in a suitable container before being placed in the retort to make it less awkward for the attendants to manage. They usually supply pressed cardboard boxes for a nominal fee if the customer does not wish to purchase a coffin.

Next to the chapel was the room where the bodies were cremated. Called the committal room, it contained four retorts behind large wooden doors. The body is placed in large, metal drawers and incinerated. The cremated remains usually weigh from five to seven pounds and contain many bone fragments. In England, the bones are pulverized, but that is not an approved method in the United States. A metal identification tag is put on each body before it is burned.

When our guide opened one of the retorts to show us the ashes of a recently cremated body, the students worried about invading the privacy of the family of the deceased. Assured that this was impossible since they didn't know the name of the family, the young people went on to discuss their own feelings about cremation versus burial.

Jonathan felt burials were a total waste of money and space. "What's the sense of being buried if you know your body is going to rot? Burning it is more economical and uses up the least amount of space. I don't want to take up space where someone could be living."

"Maybe it's just me," Ann Marie replied, "but I would find it frightening not to be able to go to the cemetery to visit the grave of someone who died. There has to be a sense of continuity. Otherwise your life ends, and you're thrown out."

"In Indian societies, burial grounds are sacred," Bill said. "Societies through the ages have special feelings about where their dead are placed. It's a part of human nature to pay homage to death in some way."

"We're running out of land to bury people in," Jonathan said. "I think in the future everyone should be cremated so the land can be used for the living. We have to be realistic."

Allen disagreed. "I wouldn't want to be cremated. You can't say, 'Sorry, there's no room, we can't bury you. You have to be cremated.' I realize there's a shortage of land, but there has to be a compromise for people like me who want to be buried."

"Maybe you should only be allowed to rent land in a cemetery," Janet said. "And after a certain length of time, they could bury someone else on top of your grave."

Modern societies are coping with this problem in a variety of ingenious ways. In many cities there are now community mausoleums. In Manhattan, for instance, all the cemeteries are filled except Trinity Church cemetery which is building a 5,100-space, high-rise mausoleum with niches for cremated remains and crypts for bodies.

In Brazil there is a thirty-nine story mausoleum, with vaults costing $1,000 each. In Nashville, a twenty-two story mausoleum provides your loved ones with separate bedrooms, not coffins, behind windows, and each room can be decorated in any style desired. Early American is popular, though some prefer French Provincial. You take an elevator to visit your grand-mother.

There are drive-in mortuaries where bodies are displayed in the windows so you don't have to get out of your car to view them. One woman was buried in her Ferrari. Another loved her dog so much she had him killed and buried with her. In some places people are buried vertically—Ben Jonson in Westminster Abbey, for instance. In ancient Peru and in some primitive cultures today, people are tied up in a little bundle with their chins resting on their knees and buried sitting up to save space.

In San Francisco bodies were moved from city cemeteries to a nearby suburb, now called Cemetery City.

In some places people are encouraged to use cemeteries for bird watching, bicycling, playing baseball or football, or as parks. Certain areas are set aside so that people aren't walking on graves. Woodlawn Cemetery in the Bronx in New York, where 230,000 people are buried, now has a community affairs coordinator, who encourages headstone rubbers, bicycle clubs, historians, architects, and families to share the hundreds of acres of well-kept grounds with the dead. Guided tours of tombs of celebrities such as Irene Castle, Herman Melville, Bat Masterson, and George M. Cohan, are offered on Sunday afternoons.

How do young people feel about recycling cemeteries?

"I think it's a very positive thing to have a park with a place for kids to play," said Lori, a high school senior in New York. "It's such a waste of land to bury people."

"I think it's horrible," her friend Karen said. "A cemetery is a place you should respect."

"You shouldn't be allowed to move bodies without a relative's consent," said Rich. "It's really private property. But if you could plan for the future and explain to people when they come to purchase a plot that the land would also be used as a park, they could decide for themselves."

Our tour ended at the cemetery, a very old one where there were elaborate mausoleums and beautifully carved statues, and we walked among the graves looking at epitaphs. We all agreed it would be a shame to destroy the old gravestones which often told the history of a whole family.

CHAPTER VII
TELLING CHILDREN ABOUT DEATH

When I asked high school and college students to tell me how their parents explained death to them, it was clear that most felt it could have been done better. Many adults are as uncomfortable telling their children about death as they are about explaining sex. Usually they skip the whole subject until a close relative dies. Lisa, a high school junior, spoke of the problem her own mother had. "My grandmother died when my little brother was five or six. My mother is a psychiatrist, and she *still* had trouble explaining it to him. He saw the coffin being lowered into the ground and he just couldn't understand how she could be going up to heaven. He accepted death but not heaven."

"What's really hard to explain," Debbie said, "is the death of a child. When an older person dies, you can say, 'Well, they had a full life.' But how do you explain a child's death? We have friends whose four-year-old daughter died of leukemia and they can't have any more children. I just don't understand it."

"I used to babysit for two kids," Karen said, "and their parents made sure that when they said their prayers, they skipped the part that says, 'If I should die before I wake.' Some kids are afraid to go to sleep at night because of that line."

According to psychologist Maria Nagy, who studied children's comprehension of death, there are three different stages of understanding, and it's important to fit the explanation of death to their ability to grasp it at different ages. Up to the age of five, children see the death of a parent or anybody else in their lives simply as a separation. Whether the parent is dead or just in the next room, it's the same to children. They know when their needs are not met. Heat is missing when they are cold, food is missing when they are hungry. Two-year-olds separated from their mother in a supermarket do not realize they will see her again.

Children of this age see death as reversible. "I know Daddy is dead, but when is he coming to play with me again?" During this stage, they become angry at the person who dies and leaves them. Children think the person could come back if he or she wanted to. It's especially confusing to a child this age if you say the person has gone away on a trip, because the child doesn't understand why he or she doesn't come back and becomes angry at being abandoned. Years later, the child feels guilty for being angry at someone who died.

In the next stage, the child accepts death as final and begins to personify it. Between five and nine, death is a person, a place, a thing, or a ghost. A dark room and death are exactly the same thing to children that age. They are afraid of the unknown, the emptiness, all those feelings associated with death. They reason that if death is a place—a cemetery or a room—they must stay away from that place to keep from dying.

At around nine or ten years of age, children begin to see death as a biological reality, a normal progression. They understand that all things die, and the death of a pet can be useful in helping them to cope with the loss of someone they love later on.*

Should children go to wakes and funerals? Should they be allowed to view the body? Dr. Kubler-Ross thinks we underestimate children. "Children realize grownups need ritual to face reality. They can cope with that far better than adults. I have taken innumerable children to wakes if their parents are not comfortable taking them. I go with them before the grownups come and carry on as if it is a big tragedy. And they want to touch them, and I say, 'Do whatever feels right.' They make much less of a fuss than grownups. If you teach children this, the next generation won't have all these hangups. Also, we wouldn't have to go through all those elaborate, expensive funeral practices, which are really a compensation for guilt and unfinished business. When you are dying, there's

---

* Robert Kastenbaum and Ruth Aisenberg. *The Psychology of Death*. New York: Springer Publishing Co., Inc., 1972, pp. 18–20.

a pool of all this unfinished business. Our work with dying children and dying adults is to help them get in touch with whatever fears they have, or guilt or shame and let them vent it so they are free. If we could reach the stage of acceptance in our young age, we would live a much more meaningful life, appreciate small things, and have different values." *

When she was asked how to tell children about a parent's death, Dr. Kubler-Ross told a beautiful story about a little girl whose mother was in a coma dying of cancer. She often counsels the dying and their relatives without charging a fee, and she arranged for the child to see her mother in the hospital. She explained to the six-year-old that her mother was like a cocoon who could not talk or move, but she could hear. Dr. Kubler-Ross told her it was important to tell her mother that she loved her and if she felt angry at her mother, she should tell her that too. Then, when the time was right, Dr. Kubler-Ross said, the cocoon would open and out would come—"A butterfly," the child shouted.

I asked young people their reaction to this way of explaining death to a child and their opinions varied a great deal.

"That's better than telling her that her mother was going to sleep," one high school junior said. "But

* Interview with Tom Snyder on the "Tomorrow" show on NBC.

I'd rather just tell her her mommy is going to die. Children should find out early that death is inevitable. That was fine for that little girl when she was in the first grade, but when she got older she would realize that you don't turn into a butterfly when you die."

"I don't think it would be a great blow to find out at fourteen that you don't turn into a butterfly when you die," Larry said. "Kids don't fall apart when they find out there's no Santa Claus."

"I think you should be honest with children," said Lori, the first speaker. "If you present death as a normal part of life, they can accept it. But if you tell them these fantasies, it will be harder for them later on."

"It's important to help children realize they can't cause another person's death by wishing it," Susan said. "My ballet teacher died when I was little and I was sure it was my fault because I had been mad at her at the time, and I told God that I wanted Him to do something to her. She died a few days later, and for about four years after that I was positive I had killed her."

The students I talked to reported their own experiences with wakes and funerals.

"When my aunt died, my father talked to my little sister and explained the funeral and the wake to her, and asked if she would like to go. He didn't want the first dead person she saw to be him or my mother. He wanted her to get accustomed to wakes and funerals as a normal part of life. She went because we were all going and didn't want to be left out. I think that's a good way to handle it."

"In the first grade," said another student, "I went to Catholic school and a priest died, and all the kids had to go to the funeral during school. A lot of us were really upset by it. They left the coffin open, and the priest said, 'You can kiss him.' None of us really knew how to handle it. We were crying because we didn't really know what was going on. I think that was a big mistake. We were only seven. It kind of upset me."

"It's hard to sit there and watch everyone cry and not understand why," said a junior. "You feel like you should cry too. My grandmother took me to my great-grandmother's plot and I felt terrible because I couldn't cry. But why should you cry? Death isn't sad for the person who dies. The older you get, the more you imitate the adults who cry and fear death. The older you get, the more afraid you are."

"When my grandmother died," said a high school senior, "we were very small. Right after my mother heard about it, she said to my sister and me, 'Your grandmother is dead.' And then she said, right from inside, 'I'm all alone now. You'll have to help me.' Which softened it somehow for us. It made it better because we had a task. We had to help our mother."

CHAPTER VIII
WHAT HAPPENS TO YOU WHEN YOU DIE?

What happens to you when you die? Each religion has its own answer to that question. By living according to the commandments of our faith, we will achieve salvation or enlightenment or eternal peace, depending on which set of beliefs we embrace.

Hindus believe they will be born again and again as an animal or a human being until they achieve liberation from the cycle of rebirth. Whatever sins are committed in one life will follow them into the next. A person responsible for crippling someone in a former life will be a cripple in this one. Accumulated "karma" —a history of actions which lives on after death—determines a person's future life. Although not a Hindu, Tom Sullivan, a blind American singer, claims to have been regressed to a former existence under hypnosis. While in this state, he relived his act of blinding a man during another lifetime, and he believes that is why he himself is blind.

Hindus practice yoga, a form of meditation, breath control, and body movement to achieve a higher level of consciousness, an emptying of the mind, which after many years of practice, purifies "consciousness so one comes to see the true nature of his own soul, and in seeing that, sees that it is different from the natural world in which it is entangled." * It is only this change in consciousness which makes a person eligible to be free from rebirth. The soul then exists in isolation and is no longer subject to suffering and being born again.

Buddhists also believe in rebirth, but the emphasis is on reaching a state of nirvana or enlightenment in this life. They strive for freedom from rebirth, at which point existence stops. They aim for an end to life after death, whereas Christians seek their reward after death. There are two main branches of Buddhism: the Mahayana Buddhism of northern Asia and the Theravad of southeastern Asia. The Mahayana Buddhists combine a search for inner peace and tranquility through an eightfold path of right views, right aspiration, right speech, right action, right livelihood, right effort, right awareness, and right concentration, and they achieve this path through meditation and devotion to the Buddha. The Theravadins also teach enlightenment through the eightfold path and meditation but do not worship Buddha. To attain nirvana, that is, to escape the wheel of life and the cycle of rebirth and suffering, one must give up desire. It is sometimes difficult for the Western mind to accept

* Ninian Smart. *The Long Search.* Boston: Little, Brown and Company, 1977.

the detachment considered the ideal by Buddhists, and indeed the Theravadins believe achieving nirvana is possible only to a few—usually monks—who devote their lives to reaching this state of mindfulness, or self-awareness, through Yoga and other methods of meditation.

The Buddhist philosophy teaches that everything changes, that there is no central soul, no permanent ego, but that we are each a continually changing pattern of actions. When we die, if we have achieved nirvana, we disappear entirely. Even the Buddha left only a footprint on a mountain. To the Buddhist, "death marks the boundary of one bundle of impermanent events." *

Like the Buddhists, Jews concentrate on life on earth, not after death. A good, pious life is reward in itself. The Ten Commandments laid down by Moses in the Old Testament set the rules for living. In addition, to live peacefully among men, to celebrate the glory of God and appreciate His goodness each day, to follow the restrictions of the Sabbath and not travel after sundown on Friday until sundown on Saturday, to follow dietary laws that are reminders of the solidarity and pride of the Jewish heritage, is to live a good life, and that is enough. The pious life is an example to others so there is no need to attempt to convert them. Jews believe that a Messiah will some day bring the kingdom of God to earth, and all will be

---

* Ninian Smart. *The Long Search*. Boston: Little, Brown and Company, 1977.

redeemed and sanctified. A rich religion, unified by tradition, Judaism stays strong in its belief in the goodness of God and man.

Christianity grew out of Judaism and shares much of the heritage of Jewish tradition. The Old Testament with its stories of Moses leading his people out of Egypt to the Promised Land, Noah and the flood, David and Solomon, and the creation of Adam and Eve in the Garden of Eden is shared by Christians and Jews. Jesus Christ himself was a Jew and Christianity was first considered a new form of Judaism.

To Christians, however, life on earth was only a preparation for resurrection after death and eternal happiness in heaven with Christ, whom they believe to be the son of God. Eternal damnation and punishment was the price for a wicked life.

Ideas of heaven and hell vary from person to person and from sect to sect, each claiming the true interpretation of Christ's teaching. Christianity is based on the belief that Christ is the son of God, born to a virgin, who came to earth to save mankind. He was crucified and rose again after His death. His disciples spread the word of His resurrection, and the Christian religion was born. Rules of conduct were determined by the Pope in Rome and by the Eastern Orthodox Church, which split off from the Roman Catholic Church. An easy way to get to heaven during the Middle Ages was by buying indulgences from a priest, who erased your sins and eased your way through the pearly gates.

Martin Luther objected to practices like this, and his break with the Catholic Church resulted in Protestantism and the subsequent proliferation of sects, each with its own road to salvation and life after death.

The Calvinists, Presbyterians, Dutch Reformed, and Huguenots followed a strict path to eternal peace. John Calvin believed that no matter what we do in this life, it doesn't really matter because we're all predestined for salvation or doom. Kinder Protestants, such as the Wesley brothers, founders of the Methodist sect, believed that each person could save himself or herself through prayers and good works. Lutherans and Episcopalians follow their own variations on the path to eternity. Baptists, members of the largest sect in the United States after Catholicism, must be baptized as adults by total immersion to be "born again" and insure salvation. Unitarians do not believe in the Trinity of the Father, Son, and Holy Ghost, as they do not accept the divinity of Jesus Christ, and strictly speaking, are not really Christians. Many Unitarians, indeed, do not believe in either God or a life after death.

But surely the best place to go when you die is the Paradise described in the Koran, the holy book of Islam. If you are a faithful Muslim, following the laws of Allah as revealed in the Koran by the prophet Muhammed, you will enter a heaven of luxury and comfort, be served wine which won't give you a hangover, eat delicious fruits and pheasants, and best of all, make love to beautiful women who remain virgins forever. The Five Pillars of Islam are the Muslim's guide to achieving this Paradise. You must pray five times a day in the direction of Mecca, make a pilgrimage to Mecca, give up alcohol and pork, and most important, worship only Allah as the one true God.

Among tribes in the South Pacific or Africa, you might become an intermediary between the living and the gods when you die. Your living descendants would still provide you with your favorite food and drink so you will protect their houses and families from evil spirits. You will have a useful purpose after death and be even more important when dead than alive.

Nobody really knows what happens when we die, of course, but some people who have mistakenly been pronounced clinically dead and then revived tell stories that are considered by some to depict after-death experiences, but by others to be hallucinations resulting from oxygen deprivation. Their stories, as reported by Dr. Raymond Moody, a psychiatrist, in his book, *Life After Life*, were startlingly similar in detail. The patient told of leaving his or her body and watching efforts used to revive him from above. Subjects felt no pain, but often heard a buzzing or whirring sound and then found themselves in a long dark, tunnel-like passageway. Many subjects were aware of an incredibly warm and loving light, which some called God, or Christ, or Love, depending on their religious background. They communicated with this being in a non-verbal way, as if exchanging thoughts in a universal language. Then their entire life appeared before them, and they understood the effect their actions had had on others. No one felt condemned for any wrongdoing, however, only an understanding of the happiness or unhappiness they had caused others. Persons who had attempted suicide would see what his or her life would have been like in the future, and they would become aware of the pain and suffering caused by their actions.

Next, the person saw somebody who had already died waiting to welcome him or her to the next world. All reported feeling such peace and deep contentment that they didn't want to come back, but they were told it was not time for them to die, and that they must return to their bodies.

Wally Cameron is a young Canadian who almost died and came back. He talked about his experience on the Phil Donahue show. Whether he really crossed the threshold into the next life, as he believes, or was only hallucinating, no one can say, but it certainly is a fascinating story. "I fell on my head and cracked my skull in four places. My heart stopped for twenty minutes. Everything went black. I heard a weird, irritating noise in my head. I left my body and down below I could see the priest giving me last rites. I looked like a used car I didn't want any more. I noticed I needed a haircut. A feeling of acceptance came over me—the most unbelievable feeling I've ever had in my life. Peaceful. I started following this light and I remember coming to a wooded area in a tunnel. I felt good. The light stopped at a wooden door. I remember putting my hand on the door and thinking, 'Is this heaven or hell?'

"I opened the door and my father was standing there. He had died two years before. I was so happy to see him, but to him, it was just like he'd seen me last week. I was in a room with huge columns and there was another room I wanted to go into. My dad said we had to sit down first and talk. We sat down at a table and somebody brought us a tray and two silver goblets. I took a drink of something that was a blood-red liquid, and I can't describe the taste because I've never had anything like that before. That's when I saw my life on the top of the table start to go down before me and boy was I embarrassed in some parts. Then my dad said, 'I think you should go back now,' but I didn't want to go back. He said, 'Shouldn't you look after Chris?'—that's my girlfriend. I remembered I had a lot to do. I said, 'Dad, I've got to go, I'll see you next time,' and he said, 'For sure you will.' Like a flash—wham—I sat up in bed, pulled out the tube in me and started yelling, 'I've got to get out of here.' I'll never be afraid of death again."

Dr. Kubler-Ross discovered the same sequence of events when she talked to her patients who returned from near-death experiences. She wrote the foreword to Dr. Moody's book, confirming his findings. "We have to have the courage to open new doors and admit that our present-day scientific tools are inadequate for many of these investigations," she says.*

Although many people disagree with her, Dr. Kubler-Ross has no doubt whatsoever that there is a life after this one because of the similar experiences of hundreds of people. She talks about one accident involving a family of five in which the mother and the youngest boy were killed immediately. The father and the two other children were in the hospital. One of the children, a little girl, was dying. Dr. Kubler-Ross went to sit with her. The child was very restless and anxious, and all of a sudden she became very calm and said, "It's all right now. Mommy and Buddy are here." Buddy was her little brother who had died at the scene of the accident, but there was no way she could have known that. She died soon afterward. "They never make a mistake about which person died," Dr. Kubler-Ross says.

Dr. Moody began to discover corroboration of his work in the writings of other cultures. Plato, for instance, wrote about the separation of the body and soul at death in dialogues such as *Phaedo, Gorgias,* and *The Republic.* He believed that the soul is imprisoned in the body at birth, and that death is the release of the soul into an awakened, reborn state. He, too, wrote of passageways, judgment days, and the liberation of death.

In *The Tibetan Book of the Dead,* written in the

* Raymond A. Moody. *Life After Life.* New York: Bantam Books, 1976, p. 2.

8th century, A.D., Moody found remarkable similarities to his own findings. This book, read to the dying patient and relatives, describes the out-of-body sensation, a bright light, a feeling of happiness and love, and a mirror in which a person's whole life is reflected.

Many people believe there are logical explanations for the experiences reported by Dr. Moody's and Dr. Kubler-Ross' patients, including drug-induced hallucinations, lack of oxygen to the brain, various neurological malfunctions, and psychological phenomena such as hallucinations caused by isolation. They do not accept these accounts as proof of life after death, but Dr. Moody does not claim that. He finds the similarity in so many hundreds of cases a remarkable coincidence, but leaves the conclusion up to the reader.

I talked to a group of high school students just after they saw the movie *Beyond and Back,* based on Dr. Moody's findings, which showed a number of people leaving their bodies after being pronounced dead, following a figure down a long passageway and greeting a loved relative at the end. Most of the teenagers I spoke to found the movie boring but were convinced that Dr. Moody's patients were reporting what they really believed they experienced.

"My father had a similar experience," said one high school senior. "He had three heart attacks and was pronounced dead three times. He didn't see a tunnel or Jesus, but he said he did remember a grassy field and sunshine. He remembered being totally peaceful and not wanting to come back. He says he's not afraid to die any more, and that life means a lot more to him. Before this, he didn't care if he lived or died, but he's a different man now. He's quieter, calmer."

Peter was skeptical of Dr. Moody's findings. "I think death is what you expect it to be. If people are religious, they will see Christ or God waiting for them. Most people have some religious training when they're little, even if they grow up to be an atheist."

"There are a lot of things that can't be explained," said Sarah, another high school student. "They study ESP experiences at universities all over the world. Whether it's religious, supernatural, mystical, or whatever, something's there that we don't yet understand. Kirlian photography, for instance. They've photographed a halo of light around a person's hand. The halo changes in appearance when the person is angry, or calm, or excited. Nobody can explain it, but it can be photographed."

Can you escape death entirely? There are people who pay $15,000, plus a maintenance fund to various cryonics societies to be frozen at the moment of death, with the hope that they can be thawed out and restored to life some time in the future when the cure for their disease is discovered.

Though no human being has ever been frozen and brought back, scientists have been able to lower the body temperature of rats drastically and then successfully revive the clinically dead animals later. Cattle breeders have been able to freeze the sperm from prize bulls and years later artificially inseminate cows to produce better beef. Human sperm can be frozen for years and used later to fertilize an ovum.

The shortage of organs for transplants can be alleviated by freezing available organs immediately after death, to be used later for successful transplants. Kidneys are in especially short supply right now, mainly because they must be transplanted immediately after the death of the donor. Some day, thanks to cryobiology, we will have banks of kidneys, pancreases, and other organs now in short supply. At the moment 45,000 people in this country suffer from kidney disease, and there are only 800 dialysis centers available. The government is concerned with the high Medicare and Medicaid costs connected with dialysis and may have to reduce payments. The technique of freezing organs could increase the life span of thousands.

Most scientists believe we won't be ready to revive human beings who have been frozen in the foreseeable future, but twenty optimistic people have had their bodies frozen anyway. After being filled with antifreeze, their bodies were placed in a plastic bag. They were then wrapped in layers of tinfoil and fiberglass and placed in a steel capsule which is then filled with liquid nitrogen and frozen to a temperature of 273 degrees Fahrenheit below zero. The only guarantee they are offered is that they have a better chance of coming back after freezing than from the grave or the crematorium. The motto of the cryonics society is "Never Say Die."

Some interesting legal problems arise here. Can the person frozen in a capsule own property? Can heirs still inherit their estates if they plan to come back? Suppose the money they have provided for the maintenance of their frozen state is used up and all their relatives have died? Who will pay to keep them encapsulated?

There may be a time when doctors will be able to replace all defective organs. Even now, they're talking about implantation of a battery-powered or nuclear-fueled heart within the next ten years. Scientists believe it is possible to slow down the aging process with drugs, hormones, restriction of diet during the first half of life to retard maturity, and lowering of body temperatures. In certain parts of Ecuador many of the inhabitants already live to be over 100. There is a theory that living and working at high altitudes strengthens the heart and prolongs their lives.

But no matter how long scientists manage to keep us alive in the future, we must all die sometime, and of course there is no answer to the question: What happens to you when you die? That it is still the most intriguing and the most frightening question for all of us, partly explains the surge of interest in the subject in the last few years. As a high school student said, "Talking about death takes away some of the fear I have about it." And that really is the main purpose of this book.

CHAPTER IX
CONCLUSION

Though death is a grim subject for a book, there have been many encouraging developments in recent years. The most important of these is an increasing willingness to talk about a forbidden subject. When an hour-long TV series like the "Lou Grant Show" devotes the whole program to the story of a woman dying of leukemia who wants to talk about it to her son, and the script sounds like it could have been written by Dr. Kubler-Ross, times have definitely changed.

Thanks to Dr. Kubler-Ross and others, the dying are no longer neglected and ignored. Doctors and nurses are trained to recognize patients' anger and withdrawal as stages of dying. Hospice teams work with patients and their families to allow the terminally ill to spend their last hours at home, surrounded by people they love, free of pain and at peace. No one need spend his or her last days in agony.

Because of the efforts of Maggie Kuhn and her Gray Panthers a healthy new militant spirit among the elderly has improved life for the aged and for us all as we approach old age. Increases in Social Security benefits and improvements in health care are important developments brought about by a new awareness of the problems of the elderly.

There seems to be a growing sympathy for the plight of those who wish to die, either because of a cruelly disabling illness or as a result of extreme emotional agony. Especially among the young the feeling seems to be, "If people want to die, let them. Why should others interfere?" A brilliant play by Brian Clark called *Whose Life Is It Anyway?* presents a moving and effective argument for allowing a young sculptor, completely paralyzed from the neck down in an accident, to die. The young man argues with doctors that an active, imaginative mind without a body to carry out the longing to create is useless. And though the doctor argues for life, as it is his obligation and instinct to do, a compassionate judge orders treatment stopped.

Equally agonizing for doctors and society is the question of whether to use extraordinary means to keep a patient alive when his or her brain has ceased to function. Pulling the plug is a modern dilemma that raises ethical and moral questions we must all confront.

No longer do people seem content to leave medical decisions solely in the hands of doctors. The more sophisticated laypersons want to know what exactly is wrong with them, the alternative treatments, and what chance they have to survive. They are asking questions about their own bodies and demanding full and careful answers they can understand. It is no longer an accepted procedure for a doctor to dismiss patients with, "You wouldn't understand it if I explained it to you. Just trust me."

More counseling help is now available to the dying and to their relatives. Nurses, psychologists, clergy, and social workers are now seeking the extra training they need to counsel terminally ill people and their families. Peer groups are set up to help parents of children with leukemia, widows, and parents who have lost children. Sometimes only a person who has experienced a loss can help another similarly afflicted. Workshops and seminars on death are filled to capacity wherever they are offered. That, too, is a result of a changing attitude toward death.

Sixteen years after the publication of Jessica Mitford's *The American Way of Death*, something is being done about the excesses of the American funeral business. New Federal Trade Commission regulations should protect grieving relatives from greedy undertakers who convince them that embalming is necessary and that they really should take the waterproof, air-tight coffin for $2,000. Funeral directors themselves have taken constructive steps to improve their image, such as tours for high school students, techniques to provide corneas to eye banks, and a serious attempt to act as sympathetic counselors to the bereaved.

A growing realization that children can accept the truth better than we thought they could has led to a new way of dealing with death with those children who are either dying themselves or who have lost a parent or close relative. It has become apparent to doctors and other health professionals that even when they are not told, children know what is going on. They sense a difference in the behavior of the adults around them and often conjure up terrifying thoughts that are much worse than the truth. As a result, more doctors now tell leukemia patients what is wrong with them, describe the course of treatment and enlist the child's help in fighting the disease. Parents are learning to discuss death with their children and to explain it in terms they can understand. Death is a part of life, and children can learn about it through the death of a pet or by spending time on a farm where birth and death are everyday occurrences. Again, a new willingness to talk about death with children is a healthy development for us all.

Finally, talking about death should increase our appreciation of life. To realize that we might not live to be eighty years old will help us live each day as fully as possible. And, as Dr. Kubler-Ross says, "It is more important to say 'I love you' once when someone can hear you, than a hundred times after they are dead."

BIBLIOGRAPHY

Agee, James. A *Death in the Family*. New York: Obolinsky McDowell, 1957; reprinted 1971 by Bantam.

Banerjee, H.N., and Oursler, Will. *Lives Unlimited—Reincarnation East and West*. Garden City: Doubleday & Co., Inc., 1974.

Bender, David L. *Problems of Death—Opposing Viewpoints*. Minneapolis: Greenhaven Press, 1974.

Benton, Richard G. *Death and Dying: Principles and Practices in Patient Care*. New York: Van Nostrand Reinhold Co., 1978.

Berg, David W., and Daugherty, George G. *The Individual, Society, and Death*. De Kalb, Ill.: Educational Perspectives Associates, 1972.

Capron, Alexander M. "Determining Death: Do We Need a Statute?" *The Hastings Center Report*, Vol. 3, No. 1, Feb., 1973, pp. 6–7.

Childress, James F. "Who Shall Live When Not All Can Live?" *Soundings*, Vol. 43, No. 4, Winter, 1970, pp. 339–354.

Craven, Joan, and Wald, Florence S. "Hospice Care for Dying Patients." *American Journal of Nursing*, Vol. 75, No. 10, October, 1975, pp. 1816–1822.

De Beauvoir, Simone. *A Very Easy Death.* New York: Warner Books, 1973.

Dempsey, David. *The Way We Die.* New York: Macmillan Publishing Co., Inc., 1975.

Donovan, John. *Wild in the World.* New York: Harper & Row, 1971.

Draznin, Yaffa. *The Business of Dying.* New York: Hawthorn Books, Inc., 1976.

Garden, Nancy. *The Loners.* New York: Viking Press, 1972.

Glover, Jonathan. *Causing Death and Saving Lives.* New York: Penguin Books, Inc., 1977.

Go Ask Alice. New York: Avon, 1972.

Gordon, David Cole. *Overcoming the Fear of Death.* Baltimore: Penguin Books, Inc., 1970.

Grollman, Earl A. *Concerning Death: A Practical Guide for the Living.* Boston: Beacon Press, 1974.

Harmer, Ruth Mulveyn. *The High Cost of Dying.* New York: Macmillan, 1963.

Head, Joseph, and Cranston, S.L. *Reincarnation: The Phoenix Fire Mystery.* New York: Julian Press/Crown Publishers, Inc., 1977.

Henig, Robin M. "Exposing the Myth of Senility." *New York Times Magazine,* December 3, 1978, p. 158.

Horan, Dennis J. "The 'Right to Die' Legislation and Judicial Developments." *The Forum.* Vol. XIII, No. 2, Winter 1978, pp. 488–497.

Huff, Claire. "Medical Care for the Terminally Ill: A Group Here Expresses Its Concern." *The Inquirer,* November 5, 1978, p. 4.

Hyde, Margaret O., and Forsyth, Elizabeth Held. *Suicide.* New York: Franklin Watts, 1978.

Jerome, Jim. "Catching Them Before Suicide." *New York Times Magazine,* January 14, 1979, p. 31.

Jonsen, Albert R. "The Totally Implantable Artificial Heart." *The Hastings Center Report,* Vol. 3, No. 5, Nov. 1973, pp. 1–4.

Kass, Leon R. "Death as an Event: A Commentary on Robert Morison." *Science*, Vol. 173, August 20, 1971, pp. 694–702.

Kastenbaum, Robert, and Aisenberg, Ruth. *The Psychology of Death.* New York: Springer Publishing Co., Inc., 1972.

Kelly, William D., and Friesen, Stanley R. "Do Cancer Patients Want to be Told?" *Surgery*, Vol. 27, 1950, pp. 822–26.

Kennedy, Ian McColl. "The Kansas Statute on Death—an Appraisal." *The New England Journal of Medicine*, Vol. 285, 1971, pp. 946–50.

Klein, Norma. *Sunshine.* New York: Holt, Rinehart, Winston, 1975.

Kron, Joan. "Designing a Better Place to Die." *New York*, March 1, 1976, pp. 43–49.

Kubler-Ross, Elisabeth. *Death: The Final Stage of Growth.* Englewood Cliffs, N.J.: Prentice-Hall, Inc., 1975.

Kubler-Ross, Elisabeth. *On Death and Dying.* New York: Macmillan Publishing Co., Inc., 1969.

Kubler-Ross, Elisabeth. *Questions and Answers on Death and Dying.* New York: Macmillan Publishing Co., Inc., 1974.

Kuhn, Margaret E. "Gray Panther Thoughts on Ageism, Health Care and Worklife." *Unpublished essay available from The Gray Panthers*, 3700 Chestnut St., Philadelphia, Pa.

Kuhn, Margaret E. "Why Old and Young Should Live Together." *Gray Panther Network*, January, 1979, p. 6.

Lepp, Ignace. *Death and Its Mysteries.* New York: Macmillan Publishing Co., Inc., 1968.

Lifton, Robert Jay, and Olson, Eric. *Living and Dying.* New York: Praeger, 1974.

May, William F. "The Sacral Power of Death in Contemporary Experience." *Social Research*, Vol. 39, Autumn 1972, pp. 463–88.

Mitford, Jessica. *The American Way of Death.* New York: Simon & Schuster, 1963.

Moody, Raymond A., Jr. *Life After Life*. New York: Bantam Books, Inc., 1976.

Morison, Robert S. "Death: Process or Event?" *Science*, Vol. 173, August 20, 1971, pp. 694–702.

Oken, Donald. "What to Tell Cancer Patients—A Study of Medical Attitudes." *The Journal of the American Medical Association*, Vol. 175. No. 13, April 1, 1961, pp. 1120–1128.

Outka, Gene. "Social Justice and Equal Access to Health Care." *The Journal of Religious Ethics*, Vol. 2, Spring 1974, pp. 11–32.

Peck, Richard. *Dreamland Lake*. New York: Holt, Rinehart, Winston, 1973.

Portwood, Doris. "A Right to Suicide?" *Psychology Today*, January, 1978, pp. 66–76.

Rosenthal, Ted. *How Could I Not Be Among You*. (Film)

Rudolph, Marguerita. *Should the Children Know?* New York: Schocken Books, 1978.

Schiff, Harriet Sarnoff. *The Bereaved Parent*. New York: Crown Publishers, Inc., 1977.

Smart, Ninian. *The Long Search*. Boston: Little, Brown and Company, 1977.

Smith, Huston. *The Religions of Man*. New York: Harper & Row, 1958.

Stein, Sara Bonnet. *About Dying*. New York: Walker & Co., 1974.

Stevenson, Ian. *Twenty Cases Suggestive of Reincarnation*. Charlottesville: University Press of Virginia, 1974.

Stoddard, Sandol. *The Hospice Movement: A Better Way of Caring for the Dying*. Briarcliff Manor: Stein and Day, 1978.

Sullivan, Michael T. "The Dying Person—His Plight and His Right." *New England Law Review*, Vol. 8, Spring 1973, pp. 197–216.

Toynbee, Arnold. *Man's Concern with Death*. New York: McGraw Hill Book Company, 1968.

Veatch, Robert M. "Choosing Not to Prolong Dying." *Medical Dimensions*. December, 1972.

Veatch, Robert. *Death, Dying, and the Biological Revolution—Our Last Chance for Responsibility*. New Haven: Yale University Press, 1976.

Woodford, Peggy. *Please Don't Go*. New York: Dutton, 1973.

INDEX

Paxton, Tom, 14
Peck, Richard, 15
People's Republic of China, 24–25, 30
Phaedo, 91
Plato, 91
Please Don't Go, 15
Polynesians, 69
Pregnancy, 41, 47
Presbyterians, 87
Protestants, 47, 67–68, 87
Psychiatrists, 2, 16, 50, 51, 77
Psychologists, 2, 5, 20, 55, 56, 65, 99

Quakers, 67
Questions and Answers on Death and Dying, 5
Quinlan, Karen Ann, 33, 37–38

Rape, 2
Reincarnation, 11, 53, 83–84
Religion, 6, 9, 83
  Egyptian, ancient, 68–69
Republic, The, 91
Retired Professional Action Group, 26
Retirement, 24–26, 30
Right to Die Laws, 40–42
Rosenthal, Ted, 4–5, 21–22, 44–45

Sabbaticals, 30
St. Christopher's Hospice, London, 5, 31
Saunders, Cicely, 31
Senility, 27
Simon and Garfunkel, 14
Social Security, 26, 98
Social workers, 2, 5, 20, 31, 36, 99
Sociologists, 2, 56
Solomon, King, 86
Spouse, Death of a, 21, 27, 39–40
Stein, Sarah Bonnet, 15
Stevenson, Robert, 13–16
Study Guide for a Mini-Course on Death, 15
Suicide
  aged, of the, 24, 50
  preventive measures, 57–59
  psychological theories of, 54–56
  teenage, 2, 10, 48–53
Sullivan, Tom, 83
Sunshine, 15

Teachers, 2, 6, 13, 16, 52
Television, 2
Thanatologists, 2
Tibetan Book of the Dead, The, 91–92
Transvestism, 2

Unitarians, 67, 87

ABOUT THE AUTHOR

Mary McHugh is the author of *The Woman Thing*, a widely acclaimed book about feminism for young readers, as well as several career guidance books published by Franklin Watts including *Law and the New Woman* and *Psychology and the New Woman*. The author's interest in the current project began when a close friend's husband died. Her daughter's reaction to the event made Ms. McHugh aware of the dearth of material on death. She decided to write a book that would answer some of the questions young people have about a subject that is often ignored or actively avoided by adults.

Mary McHugh is married to an attorney and has two daughters. She lives in the Philadelphia area.